SOLASTALGIA

D1566067

SOLASTALGIA

An Anthology of Emotion in a Disappearing World

EDITED BY PAUL BOGARD

University of Virginia Press

Charlottesville and London

University of Virginia Press
Printed in the United States of America on acid-free paper

First published 2023

9 8 7 6 5 4 3 2 1

Library of Congress Cataloging-in-Publication Data

Names: Bogard, Paul, editor.
Title: Solastalgia : an anthology of emotion in a disappearing world / edited
  by Paul Bogard.
Description: Charlottesville : University of Virginia Press, 2023.
Identifiers: LCCN 2022036008 (print) | LCCN 2022036009 (ebook) |
  ISBN 9780813948843 (paperback) | ISBN 9780813948850 (ebook)
Subjects: LCSH: Solastalgia. | Global environmental change—Psychological
  aspects. | Climatic changes—Psychological aspects. | Environmental
  psychology. | Grief. | Loss (Psychology)
Classification: LCC BF353.5.S65 S6 2023 (print) | LCC BF353.5.S65
  (ebook) | DDC 155.9—dc23/eng/20221006
LC record available at https://lccn.loc.gov/2022036008
LC ebook record available at https://lccn.loc.gov/2022036009

Cover art: Background, patternpictures.com; feather, Boonchuay_Promjiam/istock.com

For Amalie, that you know we loved this world

One of the penalties of an ecological education is that one lives alone in a world of wounds. Much of the damage inflicted on land is quite invisible to laymen. An ecologist must either harden his shell and make believe that the consequences of science are none of his business, or he must be the doctor who sees the marks of death in a community that believes itself well and does not want to be told otherwise.
—ALDO LEOPOLD, *A SAND COUNTY ALMANAC* (1949)

None of those emotions really get to the heart of what I truly feel. None of them are big enough. If I'm honest with myself, what I truly feel is . . . love. Hear me out. I don't mean any simple, sappy kind of love. I don't mean anything cute or tame. I mean living, breathing, heart-beating love. Wild love. This love is not a noun, she is an action verb. She can shoot stars into the sky. She can spark a movement. She can sustain a revolution.
—MARY ANNAÏSE HEGLAR, "BUT THE GREATEST OF THESE IS LOVE" (2019)

CONTENTS

FOREWORD

I think I was around six years old when I was first accused of moping. My family had just returned from a week's holiday at Manjimup, the home of my maternal grandparents. Manjimup is a timber town located about three hours' drive southwest of Perth, the capital city of Western Australia. Manjimup gets its name from an Indigenous word for a meeting place and a place of water and bullrushes. For me, it was a place where you can meet birdfriends.

Immediately on our return home I would find a place of solace somewhere in my house or garden and visibly mope. My mother noticed it and gently scolded me for being so aloof and rooted to the same spot. I would maintain this ridiculous moping for at least a few days and of course there was an element of theatrical drama attached to it. I was punishing my parents for removing me from Manjimup. I wanted them to know where I felt at my happiest and just how unhappy I was at no longer being there.

The reason for that happiness revolved around my core biographical and formative elements: the influence of my grandparents, the fecundity of their farm, and the richness of nature that was woven into and surrounding it. My grandmother introduced me to the life of birds, grandfather to the world of wood, the farm to self-sufficiency and the surrounding environment as a place of nature-wonder and addictive immersion.

The farm and its surrounding forest and bushland were full of wildlife. Quite apart from the trees, among the tallest flowering plants in the world, there was the huge diversity of animal and insect life. Australia is famous for its brightly colored parrots and cockatoos, and this sector of Western Australia had more than its fair share.

Small birds such as wrens and finches also caught the eye while motor-bike frogs sat on top of every fence post that provided shelter under the rosemary hedge farm garden perimeter. However, it was mainly the prox-imity to birds that created a life-long calling for me.

It was one bird in particular that caught my attention. The grey fantail (*Rhipidura albiscapa*), although not colorful and rather smallish, is an aerial acrobat as it catches insects on the wing. It fans its tail and spreads its wings in an attempt to intimidate the insects in close proximity to fly into its trap of a beak.

It is a fearless flycatcher as it will come very close to humans and swoop around the body. It is also known to land on people's heads in nesting sea-son to take strands of hair directly from the scalp. Despite gaudy parrots and other beautiful bush birds, it was this species that was to become my bird totem.

As a boy, I thought that the intimacy this bird shared with me was spe-cial and that no one else had such close encounters with it. I would chatter to it in bird language, and we would commune as if I had my own personal Peter Pan or Fairy Queen as my bush-walking companion. The grey fantail personally invited me into the world of birds.

Not all of my bird experiences at Manjimup were as communal as my contact with the fantail. A mixture of the intensely life-affirming and the inevitable life-destroying (watching a goshawk take out a western rosella parrot in the farm orchard) was enough to give even a child a glimpse into what I would later call the "psychoterratic," or Earth-psyche relationships. There was a spectrum of emotions ranging from the sublime to the terrify-ing that could envelop my childhood experiences of nature.

The melancholia I experienced at my return to suburban Perth must have been the first manifestation of those aspects of my personality, built around the positive and negative dimensions of nature and immersion in the processes of life. I was able to distinguish positively reinforcing Earth emotions from negative ones at a very early age.

That sensitivity (if it can be called that) stayed with me for the rest of my life. The grey fantail can be found in many parts of Australia and it is common in eastern Australia where I have resided for the last forty years. As an adult amateur bird person, I found out that the child-hood close encounters with this magic bird were simply it "using me" as an extension of its fan, sweeping and disturbing the ground so that it could catch flies. Despite that revelation, it remained my special bird totem.

It was John Gould (the British birdman) and his wife Elizabeth (ornithological artist) who first alerted me to the avifaunal importance of the Upper Hunter Region of New South Wales (NSW). They lived temporarily in the region in 1839–1840 and spent time exploring, collecting, and sketching. I only discovered this connection after purchasing an original lithograph of the regent bowerbird, a black and gold bowerbird beauty of the East Coast of Australia, NSW, and reading in the notes that this bird was observed and collected in the Hunter Valley.

Elizabeth Gould produced a beautiful rendition of the grey fantail, one of the precious few she was able to complete for the folio edition of *The Birds of Australia* (1848) before, at the age of thirty-seven, she died of puerperal fever after childbirth back in her home of London, England, in 1841. Her artistry captured what her husband described: "While in the air it assumes a number of lively and beautiful positions, at one moment mounting almost perpendicularly, constantly spreading its tail to the full extent, and frequently tumbling completely over in the descent."

Elizabeth Gould depicted the essence of my totemic connection to Manjimup, and the confluence of birds and place again became of overwhelming importance to me. My "bird brain" wanted me to reconnect to where the Goulds resided in the Upper Hunter, a farmhouse called Yarrundi, or "place of possums." With my family, I made a pilgrimage there. However, instead of finding rainforest, bowerbirds, and fantails, we encountered over 200 square miles of open-pit coal mining.

The earthly equivalent of a metastasizing cancer was terraforming the entire landscape into massive open-cut mines using machinery that could literally move mountains. No room here for the delicacy of a fantail in a land dominated by exploding the "overburden" and its removal by gargantuan electric shovels. The emotions of place were being "moved."

The emotion of solastalgia, or the lived experience of the desolation of a much-loved landscape, was conceived in this context. The contradiction between the tiny bird and the open cuts was irreconcilable and a new psychoterratic term had to be created to explain this form of *algia* (pain, sorrow, or grief).

Solastalgia is now, unfortunately, a concept that is increasingly well known in this era of climatic and environmental desolation. From the

RHIPIDURA ALBISCAPA: Gould.

Grey fantail, by Elizabeth Gould, from *The Birds of Australia* (1848)

Hunter Valley to the whole Earth heating as a result of fossil fuel–fired anthropogenic warming, the emotions of sense of place are being assaulted by these negative transformational forces.

Because its victims still hold within them a love of "home," the emotion of solastalgia also stimulates a response that opposes the forces that threaten one's sense of place. Working with like-minded people to oppose the causes of the distress is cathartic. The act of repairing and restoring damaged landscapes has the potential to repair damaged psyches. The pain of solastalgia is potentially reversible.

The essays so artfully chosen by Paul Bogard for this anthology help us navigate the "age of solastalgia." They all offer insight into the relationships between home, in all of its forms, and our emotional literacy and health. I thank Paul for providing this example of "sumbiotude," or working with others, to bring to fruition a pioneering anthology united by the theme of solastalgia. It has been my pleasure to read the wonderful contributions, and I live in anticipation of the positive impact they will have in this troubled world.

It is my hope that the grey fantail will prevail in a future state where humans reenter the rest of life in nature. Their bravado will have to be matched by humans who feel and see that the joie de vivre is worth more than the wealth of all the coal mines in the world. Grey fantails already know this.

Glenn Albrecht

ACKNOWLEDGMENTS

My thanks first to Angie Hogan and all the good folks at the University of Virginia Press who have helped bring this book into the world. To Miles Silman and the Center for Energy, Environment, and Sustainability (CEES) at Wake Forest University for supporting this book's creation. And to Glenn Albrecht for his hospitality, his foreword, and most of all, his word.

To my new colleagues at Hamline University, thanks for welcoming me. Thanks especially to Mike Reynolds for all he does on behalf of our community. Thank you to friends and former colleagues at James Madison University. A special thank you to Ann and Bruce Johnson who shared their home with me.

My gratitude to the writers who contributed to this collection—without them, this book would not exist. Special thanks to Cynthia Belmont, Douglas Haynes, and Jennifer Westerman for generously supplying essays for the original proposal.

To David Swirnoff and Joshua Powell, thank you for the continued conversations. To Caroline and to my parents, thank you for everything. And to Amalie, how wonderful you are here.

Finally, I give thanks for my friend, Hanna Cooper, who died far too young. I will always be grateful that we reconnected in time to have several long talks about living with the knowledge that we will lose so much of what we love—and so, how to love even more.

INTRODUCTION

The distress caused by environmental change; the homesickness we feel while still at home; the lived experience of the desolation of a much-loved landscape. All of these are ways that Glenn Albrecht has defined the word he created to describe this emotion so many feel in response to finding our beloved world so impacted, under threat, and certain to suffer radical change. To feel solastalgia is to feel pain, sorrow, and grief (from the Greek *algos*), but it is also to recognize that the source of this pain is our love for the places of which are part. And in that love lies the energy to defend the world we have known and to create the future we want our children, grandchildren, and those who follow to know.

When I first found the word a decade ago, I mostly identified with having a word to describe my grief. In *The End of Night* I wrote, "Already in Australia they're speaking of solastalgia, about missing a loved place that still exists but to which the old birds and plants and animals no longer come." Next to the loss of my family, this was "the darkness I fear most, this sadness at the ongoing destruction of the wild world." In the years since, though, I've found there is more to the emotion this word describes.

Part of this discovery came when I traveled to eastern Australia to meet Glenn Albrecht in October of 2019. From the moment Glenn and his wife, Jill, picked me up outside the Newcastle train station, their blue sedan packed with groceries and red wine, and we headed toward the property near Duns Creek they call Wallaby Farm, they were the kindest of hosts. Over the course of my stay, they fed me well, indulged my desire to see kangaroos, and took me on field trips both wonderful (to see lyrebirds) and heartbreaking (to see the massive open-pit coal mines of the Upper Hunter Valley). And all along we talked of solastalgia.

For Glenn, the word has its roots in a Western Australia childhood full of wildlife and wild places that made him the person he is today, a self-described "bird-loving environmental philosopher trying to understand Earth-human relationships." In his book *Earth Emotions: New Words for a New World*, Glenn explains that he has "been in love with birds for as long as I can remember," that "grief and mourning for the death of the nonhuman was locked into my childhood," and that during these early years, he developed the "sense of kinship to a nonhuman being" that he will "carry with me for the rest of my life." When he moved across the vast "sunburnt country" to the verdant Hunter Valley of New South Wales, those feelings bloomed.

But the idyllic existence his new home promised was soon disrupted by the reality of the area's open-pit coal mines. Albrecht began to hear from long-time residents of the Upper Hunter their despair over the destruction caused by the mines. He realized "these people were losing the solace or comfort once derived from their relationship to a home that was now being desolated by forces beyond their control." But when he went to describe their feelings, he found the English language lacking.

"Nostalgia," missing a time or place where you used to be, didn't carry the meaning he desired. He was aware of the Hopi word *koyaanisqatsi*, meaning "life out of balance or disintegrating." He knew of *uggianaqtuq* meaning "friend acting strangely," which the Inuit increasingly use to describe the weather. He knew that Indigenous peoples around the world had suffered the trauma of removal from beloved homelands (for Aboriginal Australians, the 1788 arrival of British colonizers marked the start of a destruction that haunts the country still). He was aware that this feeling was ancient and ubiquitous. But, as he writes, "it was clear that the English language had no word to describe what I felt."

Realizing this, he set out with Jill's close help to create the word that we know now as "solastalgia." Based on the Latin words for solace (*solari*), desolation (*desolare*), and pain/sorry (*algia*), solastalgia "rolled out of my mind and off my tongue as if it had always been there." He writes, "I define 'solastalgia' as the pain or distress caused by the ongoing loss of solace and the sense of desolation connected to the present state of one's home and territory. It is the existential and lived experience of negative environmental change, manifest as an attack on one's sense of place. It is characteristically a chronic condition, tied to the gradual erosion of identity created by the sense of belonging to a particular loved place and a feeling of distress, or psychological desolation, about its unwanted transformation."

In the mid-2000s, Albrecht began to make his new word public, and it has resonated with people around the world ever since.

The reasons why become more apparent with each passing year. Stories of storms and fires and disasters in places far away have now come closer to home. As I write this in the late summer, my Minnesota home has been locked in a drought that long since browned most city lawns. On several summer days the sky has turned a smoky white from Canadian forest fires, with our air quality the worst ever recorded. And the temperatures—normally we might have a handful of summer days above 90 degrees Fahrenheit, but this year, we've had weeks.

Always, too, loom the predictions—more heat, more drought (or heavy rains), more wildfires and smoke. The ancient seasonal rhythms are being disrupted and with them the old patterns of life every species has evolved to know. Gradually the state I love will be transformed, the pine forests replaced with savannah, the loons gone from the lakes they have called home for centuries.

And yet, for all the pain caused by what has been lost and what might be lost, there is, within solastalgia, the promise of possibility. As Glenn Albrecht writes, "I have always argued that solastalgia is not irreversible." The way to do so, he says, is through working to mitigate and repair whatever is causing the solastalgia in the first place. That will be different depending on where and who we are. But what remains constant is solastalgia's invitation to grieve, and then also to act.

That the developed world has so far failed to take effective action against the climate crisis rests significantly in our refusal to feel what's happening. Here in America, we live in a culture that—when it comes to "dark" or "difficult" emotions—doesn't want to hear about it. We're taught to move on, cheer up. "Don't worry, be happy," has become a kind of national motto. But grief, fear, anger, and related emotions are natural responses to our overwhelming circumstances, signals to us that something is wrong. As the bumper sticker reads: "If you're not outraged, you're not paying attention."

To feel our emotions about climate change and other destructions is to honor those natural reactions, and in doing so, to care for ourselves—to resist disillusionment, exhaustion, or apathy.

To feel these emotions is also to better understand—if we don't already—the grief and other emotions of peoples who have long suffered the brutal effects of oppression and dispossession, peoples for whom the traumas inflicted by a changing climate are the latest in a long series of traumas.

To feel these emotions is to better understand our collective fate and our connected response to a disappearing world.

As the scholar and Aboriginal Australian Bhiamie Williamson told me about the home country his ancestors have known for many thousands of years, "Being out here on the river—and the river might or might not be flowing, there may or may not be fish in there—there's a place where the old people have lived where you're deeply connected to. And yet it is both the place and not the place. And that's a really difficult thing to sit with a lot of the time because it's changed so much and because the ability to sustain your life isn't there in the way that it was."

It is both the place and not the place—coming to terms with this lies at the heart of solastalgia. Our feelings of pain and grief are important, it tells us—the futures of the places and people and wild things we love are in danger, and we are called to their defense. The question is what will we do next? How can we engage with our emotions, and why would we want to? What possibilities might we find in feeling solastalgia?

•

In these pages thirty-four writers share their answers to these and other questions. They share their solastalgia, their beloved places, their vulnerability, their stories, their visions of what we can create. It has been a powerful experience to read these essays and collect them into this anthology. I trust you will find reading these works powerful as well.

The seed for this book came from my previous experience editing *Let There Be Night: Testimony on Behalf of the Dark*. Published in 2008, this was my first book, and it created a path for a professional life of writing about the night sky and darkness. But it's the experience of asking for and receiving essays that I'll never forget—the generosity of writers willing to share their work. I remember walking across the University of Nevada campus with the visiting Kathleen Dean Moore and asking if she would be willing to write an essay for that book. Kathy wrote a beautiful essay that is first in the table of contents and is still one of my favorites. Her contribution affirmed my belief in the book and gave me the confidence to ask other writers. When I went to create *Solastalgia*, Kathy was one of the first writers I asked, and again she responded with beauty and grace (and anger) in her essay "Rage, Rage against the Dying." If ever I create a third anthology, Kathy, I'm coming your way.

In my letter to potential authors for *Solastalgia*, I wrote, "I am interested in how you are feeling. I'm interested especially in those times when you feel such emotions as anxiety, fear, and sorrow, and what you do to respond. I want to know how you simultaneously carry such powerful emotions as love and fear, joy and grief, anger and hope. What are the ways we can live a joyful life while still being engaged with a future that threatens overwhelming change? How can we use our feelings about a disappearing world to create a positive narrative for the life (and lives) to come?"

My goals for this book, I said, were three: to raise awareness of the impact on our emotions from living in a disappearing world; to argue that in order to take effective action we must be willing to engage with our emotions; and—especially—to offer the reader our company, to give them evidence that they are not alone with their feelings. I think of Aldo Leopold's words about living "alone in a world of wounds." My sense is that too many of us are living alone with our feelings about what's happening to the world we love. My hope is that this book will counter that loneliness and encourage readers to action.

I asked for a short original nonfiction work of between 1,000 and 2,000 words in any form—a letter to a child, a short essay of scene and reflection, a testimony, a rant, something more philosophical. The response was overwhelming, and I think you will find, full of wonderful writing. Not everyone had heard of "solastalgia," and a few writers didn't find the word to their liking. "I'm not sure this is what you were expecting . . ." was something I read more than once. But in fact, this was exactly what I had hoped for—thirty-four different takes on a single concept—and I was pleased to let writers follow the prompt in whatever direction they wished.

That said, these essays share more with each other than not. All of them, in their own ways, engage the pain, grief, and sorrow inherent in the concept of solastalgia. And all of them also have at least a hint—and often much more—of the possibility in this emotion. The diversity of approaches these essays take reflects a group of writers wonderfully diverse in culture, race, gender, sexual orientation, and geography. But they also are essays connected to and strengthened by one another. The feeling of solastalgia is widespread and growing; anyone who loves the planet and is aware of its uncertain future can't help but share this emotion.

I have organized the collection into five chapters. Each chapter's theme offers an answer to the question so many of us ask when we realize what the climate crisis, the biodiversity crisis, and other catastrophes are doing to our home: What can I do? I think we mean not only what can I do to deal with my feelings but also what can I do to help make things better?

So much of what will happen to our beautiful world is out of our control. So much destruction has been—and continues to be—perpetrated by a relatively small group of (largely white, wealthy, male) humans. But there is still so much we can do individually and collectively to shape the future. This book begins with the belief that every action counts, and the way we live matters. May the words offered here bring solace, understanding, and inspiration for action.

PART I

Grieve and Give Thanks

We grieve for what has been lost and what may be lost. And this is good—in our grieving we bear witness, we learn, we endure. In our grief we build connections, through those connections we find possibility, with that possibility we feel gratitude, and in that gratitude we know strength.

What If She Had Lived?

Laura Erin England

I like to imagine that if Rachel Carson had survived cancer and lived to a ripe old age, or even an average age, she would have turned her attention to climate change. How could she not have, given her deep love of nature and the danger that climate change poses to most living beings? Because Carson was a slow writer—she was known to be incredibly thorough in her research and meticulous in her revisions—I imagine she would have published her climate change book years after *Silent Spring*, perhaps in the mid-1970s. If she had lived, I imagine that her climate book would have propelled Americans into action before it was too late . . . before partisan polarization made Americans blind to information counter to their ideology; before people stopped reading books and got most of their information from social media echo chambers; before greenhouse gas concentrations accumulated to levels unprecedented in millions of years of Earth history.

"What if she had lived?" I regularly ask myself that very question with respect to my own personal loss—cancer struck down my mother when she was only forty-seven. An aggressive invasion reduced the strongest, most vibrant person I knew to skin and bones and then ashes in just six months. Witnessing her decline was horrific, nightmare-inducing. My raw emotions vacillated between anger at the unfairness of her untimely death, numbness, and desperate sadness. Grief can be extremely isolating; inconceivably, the world continues spinning. I sobbed daily to my husband. We had just married a few months prior, and on that day, Mom looked so strong; I truly believed she would beat cancer. I also wailed to my rescue dog—a golden-bodied mastiff with the most expressive eyes. I imagined her expressions were empathetic, though just as likely she was frightened by my howls. Those two patient gentle giants were my rocks during that time, yet my heart still broke.

I can only guess at the ways the tragic death of my mother changed the course of my life. If she had lived, would I have changed paths in graduate school the way I did? Would I have postponed motherhood as long as I did? How would I otherwise have spent all that emotional energy that grief drained from me during those first several years of intense mourning? Perhaps growing deeper friendships, making more music, loving the still-living more? And today, how much more fully would I feel the joy of motherhood if I could share it with my own mother, if her grandkids could know her, be shaped by her, and loved by her? An absence can be felt as intensely as a presence.

My feelings about personal loss and global tragedy are all tangled up in a web of grief inside me. I worry about whether I will live long enough to help my children navigate a future shadowed by accelerating climate disruption and all the attendant suffering. Will my mother's fate be my own—leaving my children behind far too early? I try to curb this fatalistic line of thinking. But the darkest feeling I have experienced in this tangle of grief came when I learned that my longtime friend, Erin, an accomplished ecologist whose children are the same ages as mine and who battled an aggressive cancer for nearly seven years, was in hospice care. A fleeting, involuntary feeling rattled me—envy. Envy that she will not have to witness the hotter, more volatile world that our children will grow into and the erosion of possibilities for health, happiness, and peace in our children's time. Envy is always a corrosive emotion; in this case it was an ugly residue of heartache. I sobbed, admonished myself for this appalling thought, and then filed it away as senseless. Yet these are the kind of dark, desperate feelings that the Anthropocene inspires.

On a trip last year to the coast of North Carolina with a group of colleagues from across my university, we visited the Rachel Carson Estuarine Reserve as part of our exploration of sustainable coastal communities (which increasingly feels like an oxymoron). Upon seeing a portrait of Carson, someone remarked that she looked sad. The comment was not made in empathy but rather smacked of critique. "Of *course* she was sad," I silently fumed. She spent years researching, writing, and speaking about poisons, suffering and death, to the benefit of us all. But in today's ethos of "we're all responsible for our own happiness," being sorrowful is considered a personal failure.

I've been on the receiving end of this message from someone very close to me who observed my eco-blues. "Don't you want to have more joy?" she asked. Of *course* I do, but not if it means turning a blind eye to our climate reality, and not if it means avoidance instead of action. I feel a sort of estrangement, a gulf between myself and some of those I love in terms of urgency about the climate crisis. During a late-night heart-to-heart with this loved one I revealed the depth of my climate grief and noted that psychologists are documenting a growing number of people suffering from solastalgia, ecological anxiety, and grief. She asked if I had considered talking with a therapist.

I honestly believe that eco-anxiety is the sanest reaction to the state of our planet and that those who are not feeling it are the ones who need therapy. That said, "The Great Derangement," as the Indian writer Amitav Ghosh calls it, is not an individual illness, but a collective cultural affliction that was centuries in the making. And Carson's assertion in 1955 that climate change "is now well recognized" is perhaps evidence that the postwar Great Acceleration included exponential growth not just in the drivers of climate change but also exponential growth in what Ghosh refers to as a culture marked by "patterns of evasion" and "modes of concealment."

It's oddly comforting to this solastalgic ecologist to know that popular evasion of painful truths and estranged feelings for those who face them is not unique or new. As Aldo Leopold wrote ages ago: "One of the penalties of an ecological education is that one lives alone in a world of wounds. . . . An ecologist must either harden his shell and make believe that the consequences of science are none of his business, or he must be the doctor who sees the marks of death in a community that believes itself well and does not want to be told otherwise."

Leopold also worried about the ways that those who see the "marks of death" communicate: "Conservationists have, I fear, adopted the pedagogical method of the prophets: we mutter darkly about impending doom if people don't mend their ways." Regretfully, I fell into this trap and failed utterly as a climate communicator in that late-night conversation. I was too tired to be eloquent or inspiring. I "muttered darkly" from my tangle of grief.

I like to imagine that if my mom were still living, she would have turned her attention to climate change. How could she not have, given her deep love of nature and the danger that climate change poses to most living beings? A first-grade teacher, she was a champion of the next generation and would have been consumed with worry about what the future holds for today's youth, including her six grandchildren. I envision her, fierce in purple skirts and funky earrings mingling with gray hair, marching among the grandparents advocating for urgent climate action. I would talk with her honestly, anticipating understanding and support, about climate emotions. It's yet one more way that I feel my mother's absence today.

Carson's absence is intense, palpable. American readers not only loved her, they trusted her. How would society have embraced the evidence for climate change and its myriad harms to communities of life—human and our more-than-human kin—differently if Carson had lived to write her climate change book? Would she have set us on another path, one that doesn't resemble careening toward catastrophe and self-destruction?

Carson's insight on the way forward more than half a century ago resonates in a way that is disconcertingly apt today: "I think we're challenged as mankind has never been challenged before to prove our maturity and our mastery, not of nature, but of ourselves," she wrote. Are we up to this immense challenge? Our entangled, collective fate hangs in the balance.

She—Rachel Carson, my mom, my friend Erin—is no longer living. But I am. And one thing I share with all three of these remarkable women is that I am mesmerized by life. So, when I silence the "what ifs," what remains is the key question for me—for all of us—to answer. *What am I going to write, say, and do to help reverse our headlong rush towards catastrophe and ensure future possibilities for all of the stunningly beautiful life and lives on our one and only Earth?*

On Elegy

KATHRYN NUERNBERGER

umbilicate pebblesnail, pyramid slitshell,
rubious cave amphipod, heath hen

The acacias shading the Serengeti plain have hollow thorns. When ants burrow into them, they make a flute of the tree the wind plays as it passes across all those entryways.

shortnose cisco, blackfin cisco, deep water cisco,
phantom shiner, insular cave rat

The scientist was explaining the symbiotic mutualism between whistling thorn acacias and cocktail ants the same week the last male white rhino died. You might have seen photographs of his colleagues on that preserve cradling Sudan's head in their laps. His face on my computer screen was down the hall from where they were boxing the last of the data.

angled riffleshell, bigleaf scurfpea, great auk,
dusky seaside sparrow, silver trout

He brought it up, like he couldn't help it, as people who have just been to a funeral sometimes do, but I didn't ask him what it was like. I once ate waffles at the bottom of a mountain with an ornithologist after she showed me two of the last spotted owl fledglings. Once she started crying, it was hard for her to stop.

sea mink, pallid beach mouse, tule shrew,
passenger pigeon, Brace's emerald

The burrowing of ants into the thorns of the acacia swells them into galls
that would kill another tree. But the acacia secretes a nectar from her glands
and feeds them. When a large herbivore comes, the tree mimics the signaling pheromones of the ants through her nectaries, and the ants attack in a
biting and stinging frenzy. Just a few up an elephant's trunk is enough to
save the tree.

Ainsworth's salamander, Maryland darter,
green blossom pearly mussel

And if the elephants and giraffes never come? After a while the tree stops
feeding the ants, and the ants plunder the rich ichorous sap of the heartwood.

web-footed coqui, thicktail chub, robust
burrowing mayfly, stumptooth minnow

I want to believe it is possible to understand each other. The acacia learns
to speak ant. The ants learn to answer. Even the scientists find a way to
ask how it is in their rough syllables of smokers and sticky traps and short
bursts of insecticide.

Xerces blue, ash meadows killfish, golden
coqui, Sloane's urania butterfly

But without the regular interruptions of the herbivores' dangerous hunger,
the ants learn to speak a kind of fear and greed that sounds very human.

acorn pearly mussel, snake river sucker, Alabama
pigtoe, three-toothed caddisfly

You could say the ants and the tree turn on each other. But another way to
understand what happens is grief. Where has she gone, that mother tongue
who used to work her way through the leaves, a lullaby that hummed all

the way into the roots? How will you live without that melody of a beast grunting a song she's learning from the wind?

Bachman's warbler, Florida fairy shrimp,
Amistad gambusia, Carolina parakeet

Two Hearts, Two Minds

KATHRYN MILES

I grew up in some of America's most compromised landscapes, although I didn't know it at the time. I spent my earliest years in Arizona's red rock desert. While there, our family vacationed regularly on Lake Powell: still known to some as Glen Canyon and the site of one of environmentalism's most bitter controversies. Eventually, my family relocated, first to Iowa and then to Illinois. I spent long hours racing through cornfields and floating on the Mississippi River, never once pausing to wonder what that landscape might have looked and felt like before it was forever altered by industrial agriculture. Many springtimes, my family would make the multi-day drive back to Lake Powell, where I would bask on rocks and explore hidden emerald pools with no conscious awareness of what lay buried under all that lovely water.

It wasn't until an environmental literature course in college that I learned the fraught history of these homeplaces. I studied academic-sounding concepts like *intergenerational amnesia* and *shifting baselines* and tried to make peace with the idea that what my generation had come to love others continued to grieve and condemn. Being told I loved those compromised landscapes because I hadn't seen them pristine never sat right with me. Even after coming to an awareness of what had been lost there, I still felt the heart pull of loving a place and the beauty it contained. To be told I felt that way only because I hadn't seen those places years before, as others had once experienced them, seemed to negate the honest joy I had felt there.

After graduate school, I chose the rocky shores of Mid-Coast Maine as my home. For someone who moved around a fair amount as a child, there was something reassuringly constant about sinking my roots into the glacier-swept granite defining that landscape. Over the years, I came to appreciate the folksy certainty of an early winter, a January thaw, a prolonged mud season, even with the inconveniences they brought to the human dwellers here.

In the twenty years since I've made this place my home, those milestones, too, have begun to change. We can no longer count on holiday snow, and regardless of what the *Farmers' Almanac* may foretell for the start of each new year, you cannot thaw what has yet to be frozen. The sobering reality is that the Gulf of Maine, which stretches from the bicep of Cape Cod to the narrow reaches of the Bay of Fundy, is warming faster than 99 percent of the world's ocean—seven times faster, in fact. There are complicated reasons for this: rapidly melting Arctic ice has interfered with millennia-old circulation systems in the northern Atlantic; the added increase of marine heat waves in this historically cold-water system has caused water temperatures to spike even higher; shallow geology west of Georges Bank holds the warming water in place like an unwelcome bathtub.

But knowing the scientific reasons for this exponential warming does little to halt it. Climatologists say that living in the Gulf of Maine right now is like watching a movie in fast forward: observable changes that might take decades in other places are happening here in just years and even seasons. For centuries, ours was a marine ecosystem of cod and herring; of lobster and spiny sea urchins. The past few summers, it's also been an ecosystem for black seabass and longfin squid, blue crabs and Kemp's ridley sea turtles—species historically found much, much farther south.

Scientists here agree that change in the Gulf of Maine is as rapid as it is inevitable. What remains to be seen is how we best manage it. While species like halibut depart, emerging species like butterfish will continue to arrive. As one climate expert recently told me, the only thing that remains to be seen is whether this ecological transition will be smooth or messy. In some very real ways, that choice is up to us. Perhaps not surprisingly, my climatologist friend strongly favors the former. He's been advocating new, nimble management plans that will, in his words, "help these new species get a foothold and find a chance to make a real living." It's what he colloquially calls a *bootstrap* model: in other words, that we not become so focused on lamenting what is lost that we forget to pull ourselves back up and work to promote adaptability in this new system.

That prospect doesn't sit well with some Mainers and summertime residents, both of whom have become enamored with the cold-water ecosystem that has made this coastline so iconic. They understandably grieve what it will mean to be a state with lobsters on its license plates but none in its coves and bays. I can empathize with their sentiment and the real grief that comes with it. But as a person who has spent most of my life knowing only severely compromised landscapes, I also believe we all have the capacity for more than just grief.

I couldn't articulate it at the time, but I must have at least intuited that belief as a college student, when I struggled to understand why it wasn't okay to simultaneously love a place and to mourn the damage that has occurred there—to hold both sentiments as equally valid and true. In the years since, I've come to understand that a whole host of disciplines have principles and theories that allow for this. Neuroscientists talk about the two hemispheres of our brain and the independent awareness they both contain. Psychologists distinguish between our intuitive and reflective selves. Zen Buddhists believe that we all contain both small and big minds. But my favorite school of thought in times like these actually comes from the Chicago improv school and theater Second City, which gave birth to such legends as John Belushi, Tina Fey, Chris Farley, and Joan Rivers. What these brilliant comics learned there—and what we all would do well to internalize now—is the power of two simple words: *yes, and.* As Second City execs Kelly Leonard and Tom Yorton write in their book by the same name, *yes, and* is about tapping into the power that comes from affirming and building, exploring and heightening. Good improv comics learn early that accepting what's offered and finding ways to add to it allows you to focus all of your energy on the task at hand. It's about creating something out of nothing and finding creative, previously unimaginable solutions. It's about the willingness to be surprised. To say, *yes, the Gulf of Maine is warming. And . . .*

When it comes to discussing global climate change, saying *yes, and* doesn't mean we stop fighting to minimize carbon outputs or to rectify the degradation occurring rapidly around the planet. Nor does it mean that there is no place for the profound sense of loss so many of us are experiencing in our home places. Rather, it is about embracing a Whitman-esque belief that we truly can contain multitudes—or at least deeply conflicting feelings. The truth is, we are all deep and strong enough to hold both heartbreak and love at the same time. We can celebrate, even while crying tears of grief. We can find new paths forward even as we wave goodbye to old ones.

That, I think, is what my climatologist friend was really getting at. He doesn't want to lose the cod and lobster. But he's realistic enough to know that what his parents saw of the Gulf of Maine will not be what his grandchildren will find, no matter how quickly we turn this ship around. What he's most concerned with is what we do in the meantime. And he wants to make sure it's as good a job as can be done.

His seems a wise course.

As I write this essay, autumn has come to my neck of the woods. The osprey are long gone; the last of the hummingbirds departed a week ago. But for the past several days, a gorgeous, solitary blue heron has spent its days in my front yard. I don't know why she's chosen this patch of ground: I live on a bluff a good mile or so from the ocean. But each day she returns and spends hours, slowly wading through the unruly sea of black-eyed Susans and browning ferns. They may not look it at first glance, but herons are as nimble as they are resilient. Unlike many migratory birds in this region, this species has the choice to stay or go each autumn. I don't know what this particular bird will decide, of course. But I've taken to just standing at my front door, watching her: a massive blue body, supported by two almost unthinkably spindly legs, that scissor through the vegetation, pausing often but never faltering. As I watch her, I can't help but think about how we humans can be supported by our own thin pillars of thoughts and feelings, no matter how opposed to one another they may seem at first glance. And I am comforted by the prospect that, like this single heron, we can remain buoyed by choices we may not even realize we have.

Grief and Fire

Suzanne Roberts

My friend Carolyn messaged me, saying she had a dream my old dog Ely was on our deck, barking away the flames.

I told her, "His ashes are still in the house."

She said, "Then it was him, guarding your house from fire."

I remembered the way he ran back and forth, barking at the avalanche cannons every winter, and I said, "Sounds about right."

My husband and I had meant to spread Ely's ashes in the forest this summer but hadn't gotten around to it. The forest our dog loved, the place where we took daily hikes and bike rides in the summer and skied in the winter. We had meant to hang a plaque in his honor, too, on a tree where the path from our house intersects with Powerline, a trail that has been in the national news this week, where single-track trails winding through pine forests are now bulldozer lines, a firebreak for which we are both grateful and horrified.

We watch the fire engines from our security cameras, thankful they are there, but when we hear the chainsaws and bulldozers, I think, *the poor trees,* then realize the only way to save our house and the rest of the forest was to cut down those trees, dig trenches deep into the earth. We check those cameras again and again, wondering if we will soon watch the orange conflagration approach before the picture goes black.

I recognize my feelings as anticipatory grief—the same worry and helplessness I felt when my mother was dying. All my usual routines were disrupted when I looked after her, and I spent hours online, searching for experimental cancer treatments and rare survival stories.

This week my husband and I have spent hours looking at the incident reports, social media sites, Google Earth heat maps, and the blessed security camera in front of our house. I've exchanged hundreds of texts with neighbors and friends, who are checking in on me daily. One night a neighbor sent me a video taken by the South Lake Tahoe Police Department. The hillside behind our houses glowing red with flames. Watching our forest burn feels like seeing a loved one dismembered, limb by limb. It makes me sick to my stomach, but I can't help watching it again and again.

With its famous aquamarine waters encircled by dense forests and granite, Lake Tahoe is cherished by thousands of tourists each year, and every person who visits makes a connection to this special place. It is one case where all the travel brochure clichés are true. I know everyone who has ever visited must feel saddened by the fire, in that way you might feel when a kind neighbor or colleague dies, someone who isn't exactly *your* person. You are sad, maybe even devastated for a little while, but then you move on. When it is *your* person, you never really move on, even if everyone around you hopes you will. We understand how it feels when *our* person is dying— the beloved parent, friend, or life partner. Being this close to the loss feels like a hollowing of the bones. It seems to me it's the same way with a place.

This is how grief works—it's the stumbling at the edge of hope and despair, joy and sadness. Grief is anger and guilt and distraction; it means that one minute I fret about my photo albums and books and the next minute I don't care about my things at all, only the trees and the wildflowers, the bears and the porcupines, the deer and the chipmunks. I grieve not my house but the landscape I have loved for the past two decades, where I married my husband in a rainstorm under the granite cliffs of Echo Summit, a place now known for falling fire.

We joke about how we will be eating morels, those delicious fire-born mushrooms; the next minute we are back to doomscrolling on our phones, as if by keeping a close watch we can prevent the fire's spread—because it isn't just about our houses but our home landscape. And of course, that's easy for me to say because my house is still standing, while hundreds have lost everything and are camped out in the Walmart parking lot.

I understand the risks of living at the edge of a wilderness, and I also know fire is good for forests, but not these megafires that burn hundreds of square miles and with such intense heat that they destroy everything in their paths. The Caldor is the second fire in history to cross the Sierra

Crest, and earlier this week, it looked like it might head to Nevada, crossing the mountain range twice. The Dixie fire, still burning a few hours north of us and reaching nearly a million acres, was the first to burn from one side of the Sierra to the other.

Earlier this summer we traveled across the country and through the American West; we followed the fires and the smoke—California, Oregon, Washington, Idaho, Montana, North Dakota. Twice we camped in areas that were under an evacuation warning. We drove under smoke-white skies and through blackened forests, the setting similar to Cormac McCarthy's post-apocalyptic novel *The Road*. The burnt-out future, as it turns out, is here.

Because I knew it was possible to lose our own forest, I started putting my journals into a storage unit in the desert. I did it in that just-in-case way when you believe that somehow, if you prepare for it, the thing you fear won't happen.

But I knew it would. I knew our forest had gotten lucky so far and it was just a matter of time. I knew we had entered the Pyrocene—erratic weather patterns combined with extreme drought due to climate change. We had suppressed fire for too long, the dry forests too densely packed. Our Sierra blue skies had turned brown with smoke by July. We had learned to check InciWeb and the Air Quality Index—our new lexicon of fire and smoke.

But it's impossible to think about all of it without balancing the fear and the grief with joy and hope. Or how could we live?

We were hiking on the north side of the lake, and the smoke from the Caldor hovered over the distant horizon. We passed another group, and I heard a man say, "That breeze is so nice."

I shuddered, only thinking *red flag warning*, and said to my husband, "They must not be evacuees from the south shore."

He turned to me and said, "Maybe they *are* but still think the breeze is nice."

And I realized it was true: the breeze felt both scary and lovely at once.

Other Rookeries

Joan Naviyuk Kane

Atiqtauraq is a term that has been used for millennia for someone who has drifted out to sea, not uncommonly on an ice floe as the sea ice transforms through arctic channels. For forty days at the end of the summer of 2021, I tried to keep my desecrated hopes up that despite the fact that I lived a continent away, my missing uncle Aissonna—William Kokuluk—would be found alive after his disappearance from a taxi ride between the Indian Health Service hospital in Anchorage and the home he shared with his roommate. For forty days I fixed in mind the quality of auric light one finds beneath an *umiak* stored properly, upside down, as it becomes its own shelter.

I thought back to my earliest childhood memories of this light—the entirety of it redolent of the sea and its mammals, a warmth so total that it brings tears to my eyes as I sit tensely in an overengineered chair overlooking a knot of streets in Cambridge, Massachusetts—for forty days. It was the only thing that could ground me as I sweltered through the soaking New England summer, trying to help my mother and the investigation into her youngest brother's disappearance as best I could from where I was, which, as the forty days stormed me through them, was on or near the banks of the meandering and befouled Quinobequin (Charles) River, or in a place where there was once a meadow, Chingsessing (Philadelphia), or the muddy head of the Atlantic lies on a knee of land at Aucocisco (Portland, Maine). I made close inventories, I denoted explosively recollected images to hold up against the vortex of loss, disappearance, extinction.

I conjured a man who could captain a boat. I asked him to bring my mother her brother. It was the wrong man for that journey. He brought me to me, instead, and I slouched into my overengineered chair on the fortieth day and found word that my uncle had been located.

Our weather had grown reckless. I wondered about the cold. I worried over the chilled air condensing down into the mossy understory of the boreal forest beneath Anchorage's swaths of homeless camps.

He was found wrapped in a blanket, dead. On Ugiuvak (King Island), our ancestors are laid to rest above the village, above ground. I did not walk there when I went to my family's home.

I never brought my uncles to Ugiuvak. On the hot, smoke-thick day I left Alaska for the last time, one of the last things I did before selling my car was drive my sons as far west as I could between trips to the post office to mail our few belongings to Massachusetts. We walked to the silt-gray waters of Cook Inlet and dissolved the contents of a box containing my uncle Robert's ashes into the tide.

I was not home when my uncle Charles passed. He was the only member of my family who has ever read anything I wrote and expressed anything at all about it. After my uncle Robert's funeral mass, sitting in the passenger seat as I drove to drop him off at home, he asked, "Who wrote Robert's obituary, because they did a good job."

I was in the room when my mother's oldest sister, Marie, passed but was unable to attend her funeral after I had undergone hip surgery. I was pregnant with my first son when I brought my mother to identify the body of my uncle John, who had been killed in a hit-and-run accident that went unsolved for many months after his death and culminated in a white judge briefly suspending the sentence of the man who murdered my mother's brother.

I was newly out of graduate school when my mother's brother Leonard, who left home as a young man estranged not only from his family but from anyone who knew him, died alone in West Texas. I was just out of college when I went with my mother to her sister Cecilia's house the day that the police found her dead, her home heated only by the oven in her kitchen. The stench of death is with me still.

I remember flying with their mother—my grandmother—a survivor of the 1918 flu pandemic in Qawiaraq (Mary's Igloo), of a difficult year of tuberculosis treatment in Qigiqtaaruk (Kotzebue), of relocation from Ugiuvak to Siqnazuaq (Nome) to Anchorage, on a medevac to her deathbed. I remember the peace of her home in the east end of Nome. I look into the faces of my sons, who have lived alone with me since we left their childhood home to their father, who gave it to his assistant as quickly as he could draw up the papers for me to have notarized at the bank, down the block from the miniscule Brattle Street apartment that would contain us for the first months of the ongoing COVID pandemic.

I remember with them our language, the languages we will use to get our land back, our waters back, our lives back. I remember them into my own mother's hands when I write her letters of the ways we are making to survive, to right what I can, to restore what I may. Qaaqsitaaq: they are playing by jumping away from waves on the beach. Kuguktuŋa: I am kindling a fire tonight to light the *qulliq* I carved with my older son while he carved his own from soapstone.

Inaq, Pikkuŋana: "Issriliuġnailat naniq atausiq kuguumazina.man. Taavrumuŋa ipkua Ugiuvaŋmiut taimana itpazuktut." What I heard that Aloysius Pikonganna said was, "They did not get cold as long as just a single oil lamp was burning. For that reason, the King Islanders were able to survive." What I find are the deep lines of dark traffic, and fragments are the only form I trust.

Without alliance, I was told, we could not fill the air with our difficult musics. I know you see no logic here, but what I have to say is not meant for your understanding. This page may be the only place I will write this down: it made me uncomfortable to be loved and sad to be loved less than his wife, and I am racked too with grief to have thought I could make sense of any of it.

A Shared Lament

Meera Subramanian

Dad used to put Sevin on the yard all the time," my second cousin is saying, describing the concentrated chemical that advertises its ability to kill
500 types of insects for months with a single application. We've met in a
small Texas town, at her daughter's house, and we're in the kitchen as she
spins around me cleaning up after dinner, words tumbling out with each
step. ". . . and there were these horned toads, and we wanted to keep them
as pets . . ." She loves to talk, her soft Texan accent laced with a perennial
excitement. ". . . but even though we were allowed to pick them up and
touch them, we couldn't bring them inside. But now, they're gone, all the
toads are gone." She pauses, "and it was the Sevin. That's what did it." She
thinks back to the kid she was, and how she'd made sense of the vanishing
toads. "I just thought we'd loved them to death!"

I laugh. She's a sweetheart. We don't see each other often, and it's easy to
catch up on the details of our lives. Easy to sidestep the political differences
that are rising to the surface of more conversations these days, especially
when talking about anything I'm working on as a journalist who covers the
environment. Fun things. Chemicals, vanishing species, climate change. It's
what led us to the toads.

Her husband is there too. He's as muted as his wife is effusive. They've
just returned from his fifty-fifth high school reunion, and now she's pulled
out her phone to show me pictures from the trip. There's the San Jacinto
monument on the edges of Houston, marking the spot where Sam Houston led the battle that wrestled Texas from Mexico. The monument's phallic
spire is lost in the smog of the horizon, the remains of wetlands and the

endless expanse of industry beyond. Their daughter suddenly pokes into the room, needing her mom, and the two women depart, leaving me standing alone with the quiet husband. The pictures on his wife's phone and our earlier conversation about chemicals bring back other memories for him. He begins to talk.

He tells me of his childhood home along a river on the outskirts of Houston. "The wetlands used to be everywhere," he says softly. Industry was there when he was a kid, he says, but he watched as they bought up more and more of the land. How a gypsum company strong-armed them into selling their home, replacing it with a massive pile of dust. He remembers how they started calling nearby Pasadena "Stinkadena" when the refineries and the paper mills came to dominate the air. And the water. "We got real good at waterskiing 'cause no one wanted to touch the water." But they fished from those same waters around Galveston Bay and ate their catch. He remembers harbors catching fire, repeatedly. Many of his classmates didn't make it to the reunion. "A bunch of them are gone," he says, "all from the same type of brain cancer."

Who gets to care about the land and what we're doing to it? What makes a so-called environmentalist? This kitchen conversation with my extended family members echoes those I've had with others like them in my years reporting on how we're living with this earth, upon this earth, in this age of acceleration, when the cumulative weight of humanity presses hard on the limits of this once-bountiful planet. Like my cousins, many of the people I met were working class, conservative and churchgoing. They labor with earth and animals and machines and other things they can touch with their hands. I had sought them out because I wanted to know what people who work intimately with the land were experiencing as the distant prospect of climate change suddenly became—with each drought, flood, and fire, with the disappearance of toads and pollinating insects—the lived climate change of today. The rhetoric around climate action was escalating nearly as fast as global temperatures, too often bifurcated along political lines.

Not far from my cousins in Texas, I met fourth-generation Gulf Shore oystermen who didn't know if there'd be enough of the shellfish to support a fifth generation. In Georgia, I rode in the pickup truck of a fifth-generation peach farmer to fields where withered fruit hung from branches because the winter never got cold enough to properly set the fruit. I sat at a table with a dogsledding father and daughter in Wisconsin who were losing their sport because of erratic snowfall. I stood on the banks of a beloved wild river with a Montana fly fisherman who noticed the caddis flies hatching a month early and bemoaned the fishing closures that set in when waters that should have been roaring ice-melt ran too low, too warm. Standing in the peach orchards of Georgia, holding the button of a peach that never reached its potential, I had the troubling sense that nothing was, or ever could be, the same again.

Whether with my cousins or strangers, I heard laments for our changing places. Novelist Richard Powers, writing about solastalgia, described "how we were raising a generation of troubled kids born homesick for a place they never knew," but many of the men and women I met were decades from their high school days and just as homesick, even when they hadn't left their home grounds. Their places were vanishing before their eyes.

I've sung this refrain myself, as I watch in exile from the East Coast as my heart-home of the Pacific Northwest catches fire year after year, though the blazes were rare when I lived there just fifteen years ago. Even the most climate-skeptical of my sources would stand with me on prairies and in peach orchards, agreeing about how unrecognizable so many of our places have become. Or perhaps, like a favorite relative lost to dementia, how they looked the same but were behaving in the oddest of ways. Barren peach trees in the Peach State. No fishing in Blue Ribbon rivers. Flaming forests in the dankest of old-growth.

I thought we'd loved them to death . . .

Dislocation refers to the loss of equilibrium experienced within the confines of our minds but also the disturbance of a body part, say, a shoulder or a knee. Its root draws on the word "place." We go about our lives dependent on the systems we've so far built, which require ancient carbon to be unearthed and burned to keep all the parts moving. In the process, we've changed the air, the oceans, the land. Climate change transforms the word "dislocation" into a literal upending of place.

The mind tilts in response, towards longing or anger or a desperate search for certainty. Because what we know about our world we have learned by looking to the past. Whether considering our individual lives or what the fate of human society might be, it is the past—the reassuring experience of seasons throughout 10,000 years of a steady climate—that brings understanding and sets our expectations for the future. Such a fine model of existence is no longer relevant. Global scientific reports have made it clear and the daily news, too: the future will not look or feel like the past. I correct myself: the present does not look or feel like the past.

This is the shared requiem that spans the spectrum from the dismissive to the alarmed, including the multitudes who crowd the space somewhere between the poles: the land is shifting beneath our feet. As the culture wars rage on, and the algorithmic news silos that we inhabit quicken their feed, could this one element be a link between the two sides? Could this aching loss of lands we know and love be some gossamer thread of connection across a chasm that seems to just keep widening? Because I heard it in their voices. Many were no less bereft than I was about the way the world is changing. Two sides that are prisms of each other, shadow worlds, the same and different. Yet we fell into our cultural camps, focused on different details and shape-shifted rationales for causes and effects and what to do about it all. But everyone is dislocated now, inhabitants of an unfamiliar planet that no longer behaves as expected. And all the old strategies for saving what we love are failing. With each degree of warming, all the old stories are crumbling.

My second cousin has returned to the kitchen, and we put away the last remains of dinner. She shows me one last thing on her phone: a map she found from the 1800s that might have been drawn by our shared ancestor. The young German immigrant rode on horseback across the region where we stand after the Mexican flag had been lowered and the stars-and-stripes raised, the blue bonnets sweeping over the hills each spring regardless. With the power of his drafting pen, he set down definitive lines upon paper as one of the first official cartographers of the new state of Texas. I've seen one of the grandest of his maps laid out in a huge drawer in the Texas Land Office, the 170-year-old document frayed. Not unlike the erosion of the world to which it refers. New lines are being drawn now as shorelines move inland, as deserts expand, as toads and trees and humans and other living beings change where they live, or if they live at all. The mapmaker, now, is all of us.

What new maps might we make? There is an old African American belief known as "homegoing" in which an enslaved person's spirit, after death, travels back to Africa to arrive at a place their body had never been before* but where they felt completely at home. This, then, is the flip side of solastalgia. How do we create a world in which we all feel at home, even as the land around us continues to change, as it will? As old systems unravel,

* See https://www.newyorker.com/magazine/2016/05/30/yaa-gyasi-homegoing.

what might we build in their stead? What new maps will we create, and can the left, and the right, and the masses in the middle begin to figure out how to make them together? Can the drafting pens be held by hands too often left out of world-making? Turn the old maps over. On the other side is a blank slate. There we could chart a path born of shared laments, navigate the new routes that might bring us back together.

PART II

Remember and Imagine

We remember the life and world we have known. We honor those memories by imagining and working to create the life and world we want to know.

Elegy at the Edge of Infinity

Lauren K. Alleyne

1. Heights

My father always had intention of building us a second floor, which is how we wound up with the flat cement roof and stairs that led, for decades, to nowhere but the wide-open sky. I loved that roof and would go up there often to catch the comforting combination of sunshine and breeze, to watch the activities of our neighbors, to be alone. I loved most, though, to climb it at night in the then pitch-black of our unlit barely-street and look at the stars.

I spent the first 18 years of my life in a small cane village in central Trinidad—a speck within a speck in the grand scheme of things. When I went up on the roof, either sitting on the edge swinging my legs a full story above the ground, or lying back against the sun-warmed cement, I would stare into the star-studded dark until I was dizzy. I couldn't have said it then, but now I think what drew me back to that roof was the tension of scale. During the day, my small province—my gravel road, my village, the working-class town that wrapped around it, the miles and miles of sugarcane fields—was my world. It was where we lived, went to church, attended school. It was snug and compact and complete. But atop that roof, I would come face to face with the unknowable endlessness of the tropical night sky. My *Childcraft* encyclopedia (#4 to be precise) on the "world and space" told me all about the solar system—Saturn's rings and Mars's desolate red, about stars and their long-past light—the enormity of the galaxy, which was one of many in the universe. There on the roof of my ordinary house, those bright bodies pulsed above me, sometimes so low and luminous it seemed I could just reach up and pluck them straight from the heavens.

What Kept Us

Nights on the roof, the stars strewn out
careless as toys. The moon, the shy dark.
There are dreams we can give to no one
but the sky, that echoing house of present—
absent Gods. *I wish. I wish.* Upon.
A universe lit by wanting.
Downstairs, everything that has ever loved me
lives on, calls me in.
And to answer. *Yes, I'm coming.* And to linger—
linger, there, on the flat roof, heart flung high.

2. Depths

I am a child of the ocean. My mother has a deep and abiding love of the sea, and I fully inherited it. I love the way I can hurl my body into it and, unfazed, it will catch me in its salty embrace. I love being tossed, more ragdoll than weighty bronze sculpture, by the waves. I love how when I surrender to it, the sea makes itself a bed for me, cradling the entirety of my being. When I was growing up, my mother both tended and pruned that love, on the one hand, whisking me off in the predawn dark for a morning swim before school or whispering to me that I should put my swimsuit on under my school uniform because we would be making a dash for the beach after the bell. On the other hand, she always drilled into me that the sea was a force, that it was not to be played with or taken lightly. *You can give anything to the sea,* she'd say, which meant that it could also take anything into its depths. I knew the stories—people, animals, vessels vanished by the open maw of the ocean. Under my mother's vigilant eye, I learned to leave markers on the shore, anchoring my eyes even as my body drifted; to swim parallel to the steadfast shoreline rather than out into the fickle horizon; to still rather than thrash if I found myself disoriented; to bless myself upon entering the water; and to take my leave of it walking backward, respectfully facing its expansive deep.

While instinct and tutelage compounded my awe and reverence for the sea's immeasurable might, in the water, I, too, become infinite. Lapping at the edge of my consciousness, touching me everywhere, it absorbs me; I dissolve—a grain of salt, a mineral speck blending into its endless capaciousness. Or perhaps it is more that the water remembers me to myself, recalls me to what I, as a human body, am mostly made of. I can stay in it for hours and hours, all other needs on hold while my body communes with its foundational element, every cell singing.

Island Girl Blues

Today salt water calling you like a devil;
it begs you to strip to your barest,
let the sun drip its hot, succulent light
over your brown body. Today, you want
to be taken in. You want to forget
your given name and become blue endlessness,
unzip your mind from its corsets of thought,
submit to the swallowing. Tide
surges through your blood; your heartshore's
a wilderness of waves, rabid with longing.
Today you would relinquish lungs,
trade in your skin for the glitter of scales,
barter your bones to move in perpetual drift.
Today is what exodus is made of—
the walking away that is really an inevitable
walking toward because: hunger. Because
the sea is no long-distance lover,
and your body is made mostly of water,
and is thirsty for home. Because you, dear,
love danger's liquid caress—
the kind that leaves its salt all over you,
that wrecks your days with unquenchable want.
Because the water knows your name,
and when it calls, by god, you answer.

3. Disappearance

Wonder and belonging. The vastness of the firmament, my twin loves of the sky and the ocean, have all bred in me those two, if not contrary, then conflicting, emotions. In my body, I am large and robust and take up space, but in the ocean or looking up at the sky I am whittled down to something tiny, finite and part of the infinite both.

In this planetary moment of upheaval—humans dying by the hundreds of thousands, victims of a viral pandemic; my beloved ocean choking on plastic and chemical waste; the sun braising the planet; and the brilliant fire of the stars dampened by smog, obscured by the cheap imitation of skyscrapers—those feelings are diminishing. Or are they distilling? What I believed to be infinite, immortal, everlasting reveals itself in our moment to be fleeting and fragile. I think of how we humans have tested my mother's notion of "giving anything to the ocean" and how we are arriving at its limits. I remember the stars are already gone by the time their light inspires a girl on Earth staring up at them. I try, too, to remember to hold myself still against the existential chaos of humanity's willful march toward extinction. Or is it evolution? I wonder: what does it mean to attend the end of our planet, our very own doomed and gorgeous infinity?

Trojan Sun: A Meditation

It's fall on a winter day
and my island heart beams
like a sunflower
awash in welcome light.
But the dizzied roses
of my small garden,
caught between wither and bloom
remind me: November
thunder and short skirt winters
mean our planet is off kilter;
that a mild day in Iowa
shows up oceans away
as epic, unnatural disaster—
entire villages razed to splinters

by wind and water—the shifts
in weather around our globe
sometimes slow as evolution,
sometimes more big bang
for our brazen disregard
than we'd bargained for.
Already, it's too late for so much—
the ozone layer, disappeared
rainforests and ecosystems,
our dying oceans, the thousand
species gone extinct on our watch.
But here, it's a November morning
and from a clear sky, the sun
halos the bare trees with light
bright as fool's gold. Tomorrow
winter returns, dark and dank
in tow. For now, the beauty
of it all fills my heart to breaking
as I head out into our numbered days.

Blue

ROOPALI PHADKE

I had just turned seven when I almost saw a total solar eclipse of the sun in western India. On February 16, 1980, the first total solar eclipse of the century was observed from India. Our home was in the path of totality.

I tried to jog my parents' memory recently about this event, but they don't remember it as vividly as I do. I had been playing with friends when I was urgently driven inside the house, into a curtain-drawn room and told to protect my eyes. I remember my mother, aunt, and grandmother in their long saris climbing up the veranda steps to catch the moment with special eclipse glasses in hand that my uncle had just delivered. Indian scientific annals record that the corona showed up almost symmetrical during that eight minutes of darkness.

This memory came back to me recently from out of nowhere. I have few remembrances from these years. I wonder if this event was burned into my mind because I've come to learn that it was a scientific spectacle in our rural region. The Indian Institute of Astrophysics had established an observational camp in the neighboring city of Hubli where they installed a flash spectrograph. Czech and Yugoslav teams had brought their equipment from Europe in a caravan of cars and trucks across Iran and Pakistan. Advancing astrophysics and the "scientific temper" of everyday Indians was part of the great Nehruvian postcolonial modernity project. This must have left an impression even on a seven-year-old.

I think this memory likely came back to me now because I have been looking up at the blue sky with an aching nostalgia I haven't been able to explain. I have heard that during a total solar eclipse the sky darkens first to a shade of blue, and then to a blackish blue color that occurs at no other time. As a seven-year-old I felt robbed of seeing that remarkable sky. I've been searching for that blue for the last forty years.

The lack of blue sky has also brought on my melancholy this year as raging Canadian and northern Minnesota fires brought "end of days" skies to our home this summer. The smoke thick and hazy enough to hurt your eyes and nose. My neighbor remarked it reminded him of Los Angeles in the 1950s.

The smell and look of the summer skies reminds me of living in India during my eldest son's first asthma attack as a four-month-old. The scars of those early breaths seem to still inflict his lungs some twenty years later, a plight we share with millions of parents and children growing up in urban Asia.

I recall one day in the winter of 2019 when Mumbai's pollution meters were recording an Air Quality Index (AQI) of over 300. An astonishing weather front pushed out the smoke the next day to reveal a blue sky that made Marine Drive sparkle. It happened again in July 2019 when one local news channel reported that Mumbaikars woke up "only to be left mesmerized by the beautiful and clear blue sky that soon became one of the most talked-about subjects on social media." The reporter went on to write that while such blue skies are very common across the United States, the United Kingdom, and Europe, many Mumbai residents were struck by the phenomenon. The AQI was 28 that day in July.

It is true that those of us who live in windswept stretches of the United States have come to expect a blue sky. When my husband and I moved our young family to the north in 2005, I was astonished by how blue a sky could get. The name "Minnesota" derives from the Dakota Sioux word "Mnisota," or "sky-tinted water." I felt so tricked when I learned that this is not the blue sky of providence but the benefit of a swift wind that carries our pollution southeast to Chicago.

It is also not just those of us in Minnesota or North America who are losing our blue skies. An NPR/National Geographic project "Losing the Eternal Blue Sky" chronicled how Mongolia's famed Gobi Desert blue skies are being choked by air pollution from new mining operations, increased droughts, and dust storms. The UN Environment Program established an International Day of Clear Air for Blue Skies in 2020 to draw attention to the fact that nine out of ten people across the world breathe highly polluted air. The UN's list of actions to bring back the blue includes clean transit, ending fossil-fuel subsidies, and cleaner cooking fuels.

When the wind blows just right on a blue-sky day, the leaves of the giant cottonwood tree above my home shake to reveal their iridescent underside. One night walking toward my home I recall a blue hour unlike any I had seen. This is the twenty or thirty minutes just after sunset or just before sunrise when the sky takes on the deepest of blue light. It was like when Haruki Murakami wrote in *Dance Dance Dance* that "The sky grew darker, painted blue on blue, one stroke at a time, into deeper and deeper shades of night."

I want to protect the blue but the most dramatic solution seems paradoxical. Elizabeth Kolbert's new book *Under a White Sky* describes a solar geoengineered future when carbon emissions are offset through aerosol injections. Kolbert writes that "white would become the new blue" as we tamper with our skies. This is also the premise of Kim Stanley Robinson's new science fiction novel *Ministry of the Future.* The novel describes a time when India turns to geoengineering a volcanic explosion to combat deadly heat and drought. They erase the blue sky to cool the subcontinent. It feels plausible to me as I've already seen the relentless white skies of a smoke-filled continent.

When I tilt my chin toward the sky, I often wonder if my grandchildren will see the shades of blue I have seen. Will they ache to see the blue hour before and after an eclipse? Our cultures are full of blue-sky sayings. Blue skies are consonant with positivity, clarity, possibility, and wonder. Pop psychologists refer to blue-sky thinking as the ability to brainstorm with no limits. Nelson Mandela famously wrote that "Even behind prison walls I can see the heavy clouds and the blue sky over the horizon."

I often stare up at the giant World Wildlife Fund billboard near my home wondering if anyone notices it. Against the backdrop of an enormous receding glacier, bright yellow words in a bubbly font read "Love It or Lose It." The idea that remote glaciers and coral reefs will be lost this century seems so accepted that a motorist could pass this billboard daily, spewing the very carbon dioxide that is warming the planet and not even register the message. Walking on a glacier or swimming among reef fish is still an abstract act for most people. Losing the blue sky, the thing for which my home state is named, seems almost unthinkable. Yet, it is already gone for a generation of people living in the most polluted regions of the earth.

Fifty years ago, the US Clean Air Act went into effect, saving millions of lives and bringing the blue skies back. There are many alive today who remember Los Angeles or New York City choked with smog and can revel in the changes this law meant to their everyday lives. COVID lockdowns also showed how dramatically the air can change. The EU's Blue-Sky Recovery Project aims to sustain these positive impacts. For example, Paris experienced the cleanest air in forty years during the pandemic. The EU charges ahead now to legislate only zero-emission cars, vans, buses, trucks, and motorcycles.

My husband always reminds me that nostalgia is a dangerous sport. Yet, in solastalgia, I may find inspiration and a call to action. I have come to recognize and understand why I feel blue when I search for a blue sky. But I have also learned to cherish a blue-sky day when it happens.

As I finish writing this essay, I am mesmerized by today's crisp sapphire autumn sky. The red, orange, and gold leaves actually serve to color boost the blue. I remind myself that it is a privilege to experience this, and it steels my resolve. "Save the Blue Sky" might be the next slogan that motivates a new generation to fight for cleaner air and everyone's right to gaze up into the immense beauty of the clear blue.

Whistler of the North

Cynthia Belmont

Under the spirea this morning was a white-throated sparrow hopping in the mulch, her beak clamped around a pale tuft of undercoat because we brushed the dog yesterday and now puffs of her are blowing around everywhere like dandelion seedheads. The sparrow had a prize and plans for it, this one bit among the innumerable textures in the forest and yard. White-throated sparrows lay a foundation of moss, then build the nest walls of twigs, reeds, and pine needles, then weave a cushy lining of fine roots, grasses, and deer fur or in this case dog, which is much softer, and so she chose it, it was perfect.

Some people believe that animals who are not humans live in ruts of mechanical repetition. But a sparrow determines each spring where to make her new nest, given her history—typically on the ground, though if her chicks have been taken by predators in previous years, she might place it higher, even way up in a pine.

Some also believe that animals don't think beyond the moment they're in but dwell, rather, within an incandescent eternal present. But I saw the sparrow with her design unfolding. Living in the moment is romantic but not practical unless you have at your disposal a trained domestic staff.

A meadow vole was running fast on the road ahead of my car in the black country night, sleek skitter across the tar, shimmering silver in the headlights like a loose ball of mercury, in all danger the vole had elected to make a go, a crossing. Then veered back, second-guessing as I approached, veered forward again, disappeared into the far verge, free.

On the other side of that dark stretch was something of the utmost value, worth taking the gravest risk, as is planning evident everywhere among living organisms, in the storing of nutrients, in the migrations, obviously, as the other animals and plants also pursue their projects and lifeways toward futures and in remembrance of pasts.

In the Wisconsin Northwoods where I live, dogs have jobs, one of which is the management of white-tailed deer. My collie-greyhound mix June thinks about deer a great deal, watching for them, listening, ready to blast like one enormous muscle out the door and into the field. They watch her flowing swiftly black and white toward them for a while, then they bolt, hefty northern does vaulting weightless as blown leaves, flags bouncing behind them. They pause and watch again. They seem to realize that she will not really try to catch them, as, reaching the edge of her self-determined territory, she halts, turns, and trots back.

They are in a relationship of some kind, the dog and the local deer. As sparrows knit their furs together into bedding, they meet across the field from within their versions of making a life, and the meanings of their encounters are not mine.

Truly, as an indoor dweller, I know very little about my environment—how the organisms around me relate, what they contribute and why. I don't even know where the animals are most of the time. I do know some of their sounds though, squirrels chipping, spring peepers trilling, deer crunching single-file in the evening forest. I know that the white-throated sparrow, Whistler of the North, has a song that sounds to some like Poor Sam Peabody Peabody Peabody or Oh Sweet Canada Canada Canada. Rephrasing bird words in English is a charmingly helpful mnemonic device. But if you attend to the notes over seasons, you don't need to add anything to remember because the sheen of this glittery twinkling cadence could not be anyone else's.

Audubon Society mapping shows that the white-throated sparrow's summer range is climbing due to climate change, headed steadily for the Northwest Territories and Alaska. By 2050 this bird will no longer nest in the continental United States, even this far north, it will be too hot, we will not hear this sparrow's voice again below the Canadian border. So the people up in Inuvik and Whitehorse are going to be learning something new.

The sparrows, gathering and gathering, cannot plan for this. Nor can I, what would I do, how might one prepare for such an absence? I imagine it, never hearing that gone song, I picture my land as a table where we all eat together, goodbye sparrow, and now there's a set place and no one seated there. How many Americans will notice their departure? But hasn't the world quieted and quieted over the past hundred years, as five-hundred animal species have vanished? Whatever we hear or don't hear, it sounds like the woods.

These are sparrows, not northern white rhinos, who have been much in the news lately since there are only two left on Earth, which, stunning fact, has led people from all over to fly thousands of miles to their compound in Kenya to witness their finitude. These tourists reportedly often cry, encountering such an end. Is this the connection we need in order to stop extinction—to go where it lives and touch its quivering flesh?

How many of those visitors are willing to cut down on flying thereafter so as to reduce the carbon emissions that are responsible for the climate change that threatens many other equally charismatic species? The March 2021 cover of *The New Yorker* features a skinny polar bear carrying a bag of gas station ice. Tragicomedy is one way to cope as polar bears, snow leopards, green sea turtles, giraffes, and Asian elephants board a mirror Noah's Ark where instead of rescue at our hands, they walk the plank.

As for me, I console myself with the fact that none of these creatures is conceiving their lives in these terms. I manage by thinking close to home, where endangered animals are not an abstraction: one certainty is that white-throated sparrows will not meet their disappearance from here with concern, they will simply move, and then they will move again, and then again, until there's nowhere left to go. All our fellow beings are just getting on as they are able, given what they've got, as they always have. Even that terminal wild polar bear paddling toward a last floating berg won't know that it's the final ice. Since creatures can only exist in situ, they may be heartbroken when no one returns their calls, but not even the only one left will understand that this means they're extinct.

I manage by allowing my life to be knit into the lives of the others who are where I am, so that I'm bound here, held in place. So that as the ends unravel, the strings pull because I'm a part. All I know how to do for the sparrows is care for my land. All I can do to face up to them is go outside in all ignorance and listen. This morning. Today.

The Strangest Sea

Angela Pelster

What you seek is seeking you.
—RUMI

Once, when we were fish, we gave up our gills. Because we preferred life over death and continuation over ending, we gave up our bony scales, our fins, the ability to breathe underwater, the ability to see under it too—we gave up the third membrane in our eyes. We gave up the ocean and moved onto land.

When we were four-legged, small, and rodent-like, long-nosed and scurrying, hurrying between the legs of dying dinosaurs in the dark, we gave up our whiskers, our noses that twitched, our claws. We gave up ears that moved independently, that gathered in sound like a mouth gathers food. We gave up eyes on the sides of our heads. We gave up a home in the night for a life in the light.

We slept in the trees instead. Lived in them. Played in them. Loved in them. And then we gave up the trees. We gave up swinging from branches, tails that grasped and helped us to balance. We gave up massive jaws that ground and crushed, diets of fruits and leaves, roots, nuts, and seeds. No need to kill. We gave up wide ribs and long guts. We gave up furred bodies. We gave up the forests in favor of savannahs. We gave up four legs to balance on two.

Then, with two legs, we gave up the wandering they had enabled—the long hunt that lasted for days, our miles of running in the hot sun, outlasting our prey. We gave up gathering berries and bugs, seeds and tubers; we gave up our sharpened sticks and digging roots from the ground. We gave up tools made of stone. We gave up thick bones and heavy strong bones. We gave up a hearth in the open, sleeping on the plain and tucked beneath the stars. We gave up waiting on the wind's sowing and the land's preferences in growing, that variety that once bloomed forth.

Always, always, always, we gave up our bodies and the earth returned them to us changed to match the changes it had made too. We gave up; the earth gave back.

We were given thin-walled, high-vaulted skulls to hold enormous brains perched atop our spines like olives on toothpicks. We were given long legs and short arms, hands that could carry and toss and catch; we were given opposable thumbs, shoulders that helped us throw. We were given the ability to run long distances, to sweat through our pores, and keep our bodies cool. We were given fire. The understanding of it. The start and stop and sharing of it. We were given tools of stone then bronze then iron. The idea of how to scrape and clean and carry, tools to kill and cut and carve. We were given the impulse to roam, to round the bend, crest the hill. We were given the desire to build a raft, to float and journey, the idea of other lands. We were given melanin, skin pigmentation that shifted with climate and light exposure. We were given language, symbols, art, stories, and writing. Imagination. The ability to domesticate ourselves.

The earth birthed us and shaped us, made us, remade us. We are of it. We gave and we were also given, buried within our bodies, a default nature of change: bodies that matched the nature of the world they sprang from. To change and change and change or die. At least five other human species who lived alongside us for most of our history are extinct now. Our survival was never a given. The earth never promised us that. It hasn't still.

Once, we were prey. We died beneath teeth, beaks, jaws, and claws like any other animal, afraid of pain and wanting to live (we were given the desire to live), but now, nothing is safe from us—not the plants, not the animals, not the air, not the water, not the earth itself. Not ourselves either. Some of us turn (I turn and turn) and some of us thrash (I thrash) inside the worry of our self-imposed destruction, as if the fear of wolves and lions, snakes, eagles, and leopards has come for us again inside this dark night. But they're all disappearing. It's ourselves we need to escape now.

But how do we escape our own bodies? Our own nature? Can we even hope to turn away from a self that devours and devours yet never is full? Can we hope to change again and outrun our own extinction?

Or is hope itself only another evolutionary mechanism that once kept us alive—something we must obey whether it will save us or not? Darwin's giant Galapagos tortoises could only stand by and watch as he clunked them on the head and ate them. Without the lessons of predators, the tortoises could only obey what the earth had made them to be—fearless. Are we just creatures of hope, made vulnerable by a reality that is no longer true?

The evolution of emotion leaves no prototype fossils to track. We hardly understand emotions at all, having just begun to study them in the last century and a half, having, for millennia, disparaged and discounted emotions, having imagined them something separate from the brains and bodies that produce and experience them. But what some scientists now believe, is that basic emotions are the same across cultures and times and experiences. There is evidence that we all know and share some concept of happiness and disgust, anger and distress, surprise and fear.

Fear, some say, is the oldest of our emotions. Probably one of the first to have evolved in vertebrates and so the one we share with the other animals; we all know fear. But romantic love? Acceptance? Hope? We're less certain of these. Where they came from. What their presence means and how they show up in our lives. We are, for example, the only species who cries when distressed, and tears cried in distress contain different biochemicals than tears shed for other reasons. Our emotions are our bodies, but we don't always know how.

The difficulty of being human is that we are our bodies and something more too—animals threaded through with what we've seen and felt and known within each of our individual lives and then our collective one also. We are also our culture. If we're blank slates when we're born, then the slates that our lives are written on and the chalk used for that writing are both made of 4.5 billion years of history, and the evolution of our emotions, as well as the evolution of our bodies, got us here too.

"Hope" wrote Emily Dickinson, "is the thing with feathers—/ That perches in the soul—/ And sings the tune without the words—/ And never stops—at all." We've repeated that refrain ever since, in hopes that it is true.

Hope, whatever it is, requires imagination and is tied to the idea of the future. When early humans climbed onto rafts and headed over the waters in search of new homes, they were able to do so because they could imagine land at the end of the expanse of water. Though they could not see the end of it, they hoped for it. Their bodies created it within them. So maybe I should trust the body more—that hopeful animal that brought us here—because the quintessential nature of the earth is its changeability, and the quintessential nature of humanity is too. And yet. This body also gives me fear.

Maybe I give in to fear more than I should, but the air was so thick with forest ash this summer, so hot with the burning sun, so dry from the rains that would not come that I hardly dared go outside. Even the trees are leaving. Migrating like humans on rafts to new lands, their own so inhospitable, but they can't move fast enough for what we've done. So back and forth I go between hope and fear, between the past that got us here and the nature that past made us to be.

Once, I read, we nearly went extinct before. The climate changed, turned cold and arid, deserts grew, the ice did too, and we started to die off. Between 123,000 and 195,000 years ago, we dropped in numbers from more than 10,000 adults to just a few hundred. Somewhere, tucked inside our bodies, is the DNA map that traces every single human alive today back to that group who survived.

We've been here before, and our bodies know it, our brains and emotions do too; we recognize this place of threat. The fear and despair, hope and imagination it calls us too.

"I've heard it in the chillest land—/ And on the strangest Sea—/ Yet—never—in Extremity, / It asked a crumb—of me."

We are afloat on the strangest sea. Made of that strangeness even while it threatens to drown us. My body is a raft. We are rafts made of hope, yes, but more than that too. We know fear like all the other animals. And maybe our shared fear points to something shadowy and foreboding about this universe that made us, or maybe it points to how much we all want to live. How much we love this place. What we need in order to survive it.

Fear and hope saved us when we were fish, and rat-like, vertebrates, and early humans in danger of extinction. And despair and imagination did too. I can imagine the end of us. It isn't hard—an earth free of our wounding and a great exhalation of relief. And I can imagine the next evolution of us too, our change into something more glorious. That hoped-for land at the end of the water.

This moment of possibility rises before us, none of it yet written except in our bones, our brains, our cells, our DNA, our nature, the thing we are. But I don't know where it will take us. What will happen next. I can only listen to the body, the universe that made it, this ancient desire to live. It sounds like prayer. Like begging the ancestors to teach us how to give up once again.

On Memory and Survival

Nickole Brown

> Slender memory, stay with me.
> —LI-YOUNG LEE, "MNEMONIC"

I could blame it on a lot of things.

On my education, or lack thereof, on the way I still can't spell worth a damn. Or I could blame it on my grandmother, the one who helped raise me, how she despised antique furniture as she despised anything that held to the past, especially photographs—most were thrown away, and what few she kept were tossed in the junk drawer under coupons and catsup packs.

I could blame it on my brain-building diet of Cheetos and Little Debbies, all my childhood favorites finger-stain-lickable and plastic-wrapped. Or I could blame it on my magpie of a mind, distracted as I am by shiny baubles and bracelets, whatever's flashing across a screen. Or on being too busy, too flaky, too blonde.

Or I could blame it on that man and what he did to me in the basement when I was young enough to still believe in Santa Claus. To survive, I engaged in a willful kind of erasure, a strategy so successful it blunted out all of second grade.

Whatever the cause, I don't remember things well.

•

Take, for example, the spring of 2002: I was working for an independent press, in a meeting at *The New Yorker* on the twenty-first floor. Back then, the city was still fluttering with flyers from 9/11, so when I first saw out the window a jittering scribble of black and orange streaming past, my mind tricked me into thinking that's just what it was—the tatters of homemade posters from that sad wall at St. Vincent's blown north, all the way to Times Square before being sent sky-high. I thought it was the eight-month-old shreds left of one photocopied plea after the next, each with a weather-faded photo and *m-i-s-s-i-n-g* hand-scrawled across the top.

But a closer look revealed something else—a cluster of monarchs, maybe five hundred of them, maybe more, something akin to a murmuration but born of confetti and not birds. I could hardly believe the wild scatter of wings, frantic, catapulted by the updraft of a building built tall enough to scrape the sky. They worked their fragile bodies hard to escape the current. Some were lifted up and out of sight; others were pressed against the glass.

Ms. Quinn, I said. And when she didn't look up from her notes: *Alice. Alice, turn around.* She swiveled her chair to see what I was seeing, and terrible as it sounds, that is where my memory ends.

Why? Because made as I am, afterward, I diminished the memory, dissolved it entire. I left that meeting and jumped in a cab, and going back all these years, I find I noted in my journal not much more than the date and Alice's name.

Because that's how I work. Because it was too unusual, too beautiful, too wrong.

Besides, wasn't I always making things up in my head back then? I was visiting the city every few months, making the trip from Louisville to LaGuardia and back, and to get by, I was always fantasizing the smell of hay in stainless steel elevators, imagining katydid song to eclipse the grip of nightclub bass in the blue-lit filth of bathroom stalls.

And didn't I later read that monarchs never flocked and only migrated alone? I had to have made it up.

I dismissed those butterflies as a dream, as another something a Kentucky girl like myself conjured to make my time in the city manageable, because I never quite fit in there, never felt safe, especially after those two planes slammed into our lives.

•

Now twenty years have passed. Twenty years to make those years seem nearly nostalgic. Now there are politicians who make the president back then look more like a befuddled old uncle than who he really was.

Now there are fires, terrifying blazes, and when I scroll through the news, I see flying foxes dropping like overripe fruit from scorching Australian skies, koalas with ears burned clean off their sweet heads. A post beyond that is a compilation from another fire in California: miniature silver rivers stream from a melted hubcap, a roadside motel sign pours like boiling caramel from its heat-mutilated frame, a Port-A-Jon with its charred door flung open looks like a shitbox in the seventh circle of hell.

I put my phone down, say to my wife, *things are looking biblical,* but she dislikes when I go dark, rightly gets frustrated when I give myself over to despair, as I often do. I almost say *end times* but think how backwater Baptist that might sound, how I'll just be showing my Christ-haunted roots again. So I say nothing, change the subject, ask what she might want for dinner instead.

As I peel the potatoes, I can hardly remember what I was so upset about. These past few years, I've disassociated daily, much worse than before. Some days, I hardly remember anything. Some days, I hesitate when asked my own name, afraid I'll answer wrong.

•

Last spring, I tried to do something to make myself feel better, which for me meant signing up for a class to learn something of ornithology or at least look at birds with a group of people who love to look at birds too. It seemed like a tweedy, retiree-mellow thing to do, something no more emotionally charged than binge-watching *The Great British Baking Show*.

But even that wasn't safe. On our first day, a woman in the group spotted something high up in a tree. I saw her look hard then quickly look away. The others in the group followed, glancing up before also looking away, so I had to look too.

What I first saw caught in the branches was a cheap, black grocery bag, the crinkly kind I used to get from the little bodegas in the city. No. I adjusted my binoculars and made out something else: a black kite bound by its own string.

But then: a blue sheen to the black. Oil-slick glossy, ruffled in the wind.

Then: a sun-bleached black sock. No, a deflated length of bike tire. No. A neck, bald and gray, a neck turned the wrong way. A beak pointing down. A beak pointing down toward the trail below, straight toward me.

What we had found was a black vulture, or at least the freshly limp body of one, suspended in a sycamore. What we had found was a creature done in by the death grip of fishing line.

•

What I later told a friend who loves birds and knows more about them than I ever will was that it was an unmistakable sight, something I could never forget. But I lied.

I should have told him the truth. I should have said I nearly forgot what I saw, that I could feel my brain doing its fan dance of *turn away*, already blocking for me what I did not want to see.

•

But this time, something was different. Because a few weeks before I saw that vulture, I saw Alice again—that colleague from all those years ago.

It had been nearly two decades since I'd visited her last. And because of the virus, she'd put together an anthology of poets responding to the pandemic, and because of the virus, we were reading together, but online. From her new home upstate, she read poems from an empty room into the small black aperture of a computer's camera, and from my new home in the mountains of North Carolina, I did the same.

Foolish as I felt, it took me all of an hour to ask, thinking for certain I'd made that memory up, but just before she signed off, I took a chance, asked, *Hey, Alice, I know this sounds odd, but do you remember those butterflies?*

And just when I was sure she'd give me a confused look, she brightened, said, *Oh! You. You were there? I'm glad a poet was there with me.*

Then, just like that, my memory was given back to me, whole and real, simply because she'd remembered it. Because that's what witnessing does.

•

So that day, standing under that vulture, instead of doing what I usually do, I stayed. I stayed long enough for the rest of the class to move on, each of them looking up before shaking their head and walking off, each of them following one blissful little citrine note after the next into the woods, turning their sights to sweeter things instead.

I stood there for a long time, long enough to feel embarrassed, long enough to fear I was being macabre, overly dramatic. Joggers went past, dog walkers too, but not one of them cared to ask. Or perhaps none dared ask. Perhaps I looked intense, the argument I was having with myself blooming across my face: I was trying to memorize something I was already forgetting; I was trying to force myself to remember what I was wired to let go.

When that didn't work, I apologized to my memory for always brushing her aside. I begged her. *Please, memory. Stay, stay. Don't listen to that old part of me if I tell you to go away. This isn't about me but what happened in that tree. Please. Don't go.*

Finally, my mind let me map the forensics, to trace how the great bird must have flown into the invisible threads likely left over from a sloppy cast, lines tangled in limbs reaching over the nearby lake. How the bird might have thought it a spider's filament at first, but the more he fought to free himself, the more things must have tightened and snared. The shimmering white glint around the base of both wings, the white glint suspending one leg.

I stayed to try to forgive the fishermen along the shore, how perhaps they were oblivious to the ghost lines they left behind. I wondered if they too would glance up, see the sight, and also mistake it for a black grocery bag.

I stayed to imagine what was to come: First, maybe ants. Then flies, beetles. Then maybe the vulture's own mother, his own sister, his son. Would they finish him off, sky-burial style? And would that be a horror or a sacrament? But, no: Didn't I read that vultures wouldn't eat one of their own, that when farmers back home had problems with vultures killing newborn lambs, they would shoot one vulture and tie the body up with bright bailing twine, making a hideous scarecrow for others who thought of doing the same?

Either way, a year from now, would I find the sight of that vulture again? Would a wind chime of bones be rattling the tree? A gray rag of skin, a clump of feathers? And really, how long would that nearly unbreakable plastic hold?

I stayed longer than was healthy, my arms quivering as I gripped my binoculars, craning upward so long that when I returned home, my neck was an angry cable of pain.

•

I won't pretend my memory isn't still a rusted colander, a sail shot through with holes. But it's different now.

Now, I realize that witnessing that vulture wasn't so much about making myself look hard enough to remember but looking so hard the looking made not a memory but its stain. I understand that remembering those butterflies was a gift I threw away not because I didn't believe in what I saw but because I didn't believe in myself.

And while what I read all those years ago was true—monarchs do migrate alone—there's always more to learn. They do fly solo, but as they're all going the same way at the same time, sometimes they drift together by laws of temperature and wind and rain. A collective of them is not a *flock* but an *aggregation*—they gather in mass, sometimes in trees at night, and the right weather can lift the glorious mass of them up at once. Most likely, that day they were riding a thermal, and when they started to come down out of it, they got caught up and were pushed against the windows of that building that held me inside it, dumbly blinking from the other side.

What's harder to admit is what I saw all those years ago was a glimpse of the last of the migrations as they were meant to be, just as their populations slipped off the edge of a precipice entirely human-made. All this year, I've looked and looked for them, but I swear: the best I could do to spot a monarch was to find a single specimen visiting mildew-spotted milkweed ruined by recent floods.

•

So what is it I need to learn, what is it I need to recite by heart? Why work so hard to verify a cloudburst of butterflies migrating so long ago through the busiest part of one of the busiest cities on Earth? Why struggle to make sure I remember a vulture who likely starved upside down?

Because above me, now, I see my memories—all our memories—as an aggregation tossed aside by impossibly wrong winds. I see them as a kettle of winged things circling, circling, not sure where to land, but hungry and smelling yet another of their own kind dismantling in a tree.

Because survival has to do with remembering what you most do not want to face. It has to do with not turning away, in believing your own testimony, in writing it down. Years ago, the act of writing wasn't just about casting light on the dank recesses of my childhood, but just this—rising up to share your words to help others who have passed through the same.

What I mean to say is it's no longer just about my memories slipping from me or why. Because the trauma of this time no longer belongs to me or any one of us. It never did, really, but now there's no denying the trauma is ours, is collective, is happening to all living things, human and not, all of us, at once.

We must remember, each of us. We must keep remembering in case one day another needs that memory to survive.

What You Studyin' On

An Environmental Statement

SEAN HILL

Sometime around 1998, I sat down with my grandmother in her living room to talk with her about her life. I did this with the intent of writing poems because a workshop classmate thought I'd brought in one too many poems about my father and pointed out that I must have a mother or grandmothers. That was true. It seemed I'd been studying my complicated relationship with my father (typical of fathers and sons) my whole life and felt compelled to explore that further on the page. But when challenged to write about the women in my family I realized I didn't know where to start. I'd been around them all my life, but I only knew scant details of lives; I knew them in the role of mother or aunt or grandmother but not as people outside of those comfortable relationships with me. I'd taken them for granted. So, I sat down with one of my grandmothers and a notepad and tape recorder.

The whole experience was oddly formal and informal. My aunt would occasionally walk in and join the interview. My grandmother told me about family members from her generation or older or about my long-gone grandfather as well as segregation and what contact she had with white people. In the cozy living room of that house her father and grandfather built, she told me about when they lived on a farm in the country and how she and her brothers attended a one-room school that was behind their little country church. She told me about how the ice spikes grew from the red Georgia clay in the cold winter months. The needle ice would be there along the side of the road in the morning when they walked to school and in the evening when they returned home. She commented on how things had changed: "We used to have cold weather back then, but we don't have no cold weather now. Think it's a warning?"

I left Georgia for Houston, Texas, in 2000 to study creative writing. That was my first time living outside of Georgia. Houston felt like expressions of human ambition laid over marshland, and I loved the insistence of nature I saw everywhere there. For instance, on campus I once saw tadpoles swimming in the tire rut of a grounds crew truck where rainwater had collected at the edge of a sidewalk. In that sprawling city it seemed any declivity that gathered water at its bottom would invite life. Three years after moving to Houston, I moved for love to a small Minnesota town at the northernmost point of the Mississippi River and fell in love with that place—called it home for more than a decade. I also spent a magical year in Madison, Wisconsin, on the isthmus between Lake Mendota and Lake Monona. And then there was the gift of two years living in Oakland, California, exploring the beaches and trails of the San Francisco Bay Area. And there was half a decade or so that the endlessly fascinating Fairbanks, Alaska, was home. My peregrinations not over, there was a too-short time in southern Georgia, before settling into southwestern Montana.

In these places—heart homes—I found that though I have my relationship with them, that relationship was limited by what I knew of the place. There's a kind of study of a place that comes with living attentively in a place for a lifetime or at least a long while. Folks with a longer history of a place can make statements like my grandmother's *it ain't as cold as it used to be*. In those northern homes I got *the winters aren't as long as they used to be*. In Minnesota it was *gotta get the fish houses off the lake earlier*. The coldest I saw in Fairbanks was fifty below zero, but I was told it used to be colder.

The warming Arctic and heatwaves and thawing permafrost releasing greenhouse gases and lack of sea ice are major concerns, but I've seen enough to know the global warming trend is changing things everywhere, not just in cold places.

Not too long after I moved with my family to a town in southern Georgia a couple hours south and east (closer to the coast) of where I grew up, we heard about hurricane Irma in the news. In a few days, we went from taking note of a storm to trying to figure out how to prepare for its landfall. I wasn't worried until I went to the Walmart in town for something unrelated to the storm and saw people buying the last of the water and other essentials—the camping aisle was bare; flashlights and gas cans were all gone. And when I decided I should probably fill up the car just in case we needed to evacuate, I found that not all the pumps at the Murphy USA station worked, and the ones that did were pumping slowly. This was unsettling and even more so when a police officer pulled in across from me and asked if there was still gas at the station. I would have assumed he would know more about the situation than me.

Once officials ordered the evacuation of Savannah, we decided we should move farther inland too. We made our way a couple hundred miles northwest to Atlanta. When it moved inland, the storm eventually made its way there and caused a power outage for a while.

The next summer we moved to Montana and escaped Georgia's heat. But the following winter brought Montana's coldest February on record. It was newsworthy and concerning to the folks around us to have a month of sustained record lows in the twenties below, but having spent a few winters in Alaska, I felt more than prepared. My perspective was skewed. It brought back fond memories of acclimatizing to the long deep freeze up there where one day I waited in line to get my picture taken in front of the digital clock and thermometer on the University of Fairbanks campus because the temperature was lower than forty below.

The following summer in Montana was lovely until the days got hazy and on occasion downright smoky. There are massive wildfires in Alaska each summer, and Fairbanks could get smoky, and ash could fall from the sky like out-of-season snow, but the fire seasons and unhealthy air we've had in Montana the last couple fire seasons feel somehow more intense— and more worrying. As much as having an active young son who wants to ride his bike and play outside in the summer, perhaps this has to do with the fact that I've stayed put for the last couple fire seasons—no conferences, vacations, visits to family in Georgia—due to a global pandemic. At any rate, I feel more aware of "fire season" and fires across the West these days.

These days, I talk with that aunt who intermittently joined my interview with her mother at least once a week. I recently asked her about a phrase I heard in the Black community I grew up in in central Georgia—"I ain't studdin you." It was a dismissive phrase, something said to someone to let them know you weren't paying them or their words or actions any attention. I knew the phrase as a native speaker in that community, so it wasn't till later that it occurred to me to hear them as "I am not studying you." But in our recent conversation, my aunt steered me back to "studdin" saying, "it's not 'studying'; the word is 'studdin.'" She offered further clarification with "*I ain't studdin you* means *I ain't thinking about you.*" I was concerned with etymology, the origin of *studdin,* but for her that didn't matter and wasn't anything she wanted to speculate on. She grew up hearing "I ain't studdin you," and the word's life in the mouths of those around her is where its meaning comes from. Being attentive to a living language in one's life—I love that relationship with words too. And when it comes to our environment and the human impact on it, I may not be studying it, but I have been thinking about it intently for a while now.

In 2005 I took circuitous road trip from northern Minnesota to Vancouver, British Columbia. I spent time in Glacier National Park and was shocked by historical photographs that let me see how much its namesake glaciers have receded over the years. In 2015 what was planned as a Valentine's getaway to Juneau became an occasion for my wife and I to celebrate the conception of our child. We took the city bus as far as it would get us and walked the mile and a half or so to the Mendenhall Glacier Visitor Center to see the glacier. There were historical photographs that showed how much the glacier had receded over the years. We were aghast as we stepped onto the path of parenthood and wondered what would be our child's world.

I think a fair bit about how I walk through this world in my body—a man, Black, a wandering southerner. But I also think about the effects all our bodies—our needs, desires, and privileges—have on our environments (the places we live) and communities (all the beings we share this gas-wrapped orb—this Earth—with). Sometimes when I walk through the electric doors of a grocery store, I go through a series of emotions. I marvel at the amount of energy and resources that goes into producing all the produce in the bins, the food on the shelves, the meat in refrigerators and freezers, the paper and plastics for the packaging. And I think about all the resources and energy used to gather the bounty in this way in this place. A couple times in Fairbanks I walked into Fred Meyer, the everything store, and found the grocery shelves, refrigerators, and freezers practically bare. When I'd ask a clerk what was going on, I'd be told that the boat didn't arrive. Most of the food comes in through the port of Anchorage and must be brought about 360 miles inland to Fairbanks. Ninety-five percent of the food in Alaska is imported, but it wasn't always this way. Then I wonder how sustainable and renewable it all is, and I get anxious.

A few years ago, I was in Honolulu for a conference. I'd just arrived at my hotel room and was settling in when something caught my eye partway up a distant lush green hill. It was a rainbow smudge. I went out on the balcony to look at it, and it seemed to be getting larger. It slowly grew and arced and became a rainbow. I watched a rainbow grow out of the ground! Later as I went across town to meet friends for dinner I was overwhelmed by the number of people and the sense that though the place was restorative for us our presence wasn't sustainable. We were a burden on this place.

In my living in various states and traveling around the nation, I've been struck by the homogenizing, flattening, and disorienting effect of big box stores—bastions of consumerism. I sometimes feel lost coming out of a Best Buy or Target or Lowe's to a parking lot that looks like any other. I have to look beyond the parking lot to the horizon to see where I am. Often when I look around me at the world shaped by our modern myopic willfulness, I swing between feeling sad, anxious, resigned, pensive, sardonic, regretful, and overwhelmed. I haven't spent most all of my life getting to know one place like my grandmother, and some days that is a regret I hold. But most days I try to honor the ways she and my ancestors readied me to go out into the world—live attentively and do your best to support your community—which for me now is much more expansive than she was likely ever invited to imagine for herself or her grandson. I work to maintain connection with and reverence for this world we all share. Finding surprise and admiration—wonder—in our existence and nature's insistence is a studied—and steadying—practice.

A Return to Feeling

Holly Haworth

How do you feel? A friend or loved one sometimes asks us on an ordinary day. A simple question our kind has asked one another for millennia. How to answer simply on this ordinary day when the world is disappearing?

With my hands, I might tell them. I touch everything. The smooth exoskeleton of a stag beetle. I pick it up at the place between the thorax and abdomen, move it from the path where shod feet tread. I set it down in the leaves and go for one stroke, with just my index, of its shiny back. Its pincers gnaw at the air, feeling in turn for what's feeling it.

I walk on, waving my arms ahead of me to feel for the webs of spiders. When my fingers catch on a taut thread, I pull it, slowly—satisfying stretch of the silk, the strength of resistance—until it snaps. Drape it gently over a branch and keep going. A creature that leaves no trace is not a creature and doesn't feel anything. I feel the way forward, as I must, breaking webs. I leave my own tracks because I have a body, because I am part of the web of bodies, of living things, today. I feel good when I'm out walking, feel like myself.

Something hops: a frog the size of my thumbnail. I ask forgiveness, for always feeling curious, wanting to be nearer to everything; I pick it up. Cool skin, like a tiny prune it rests in my palm, and I can't feel its sticky fingers or its weight, it is so light. It stares ahead, sits very still. Its blood hammers in its throat. I imagine it is torn between staying frozen and propelling off into the vast space between my palm and the earth's surface. I lower my hand, and it leaps out, and I touch, unthinkingly, my palm to the ground, the dried leaves and ragged forbs.

"Our hands imbibe like roots," wrote St. Francis of Assisi, "so I place them on what is beautiful in this world." I feel with a thirst on this ordinary day in the woods behind my house. My hands drink beauty, feel the world that hasn't disappeared. I reach to caress river cane that shoots up along the creek, the leaves underneath downy like I imagine a pocket mouse's fur to be. The resinous leaves of a sweetgum sapling: my thumb glides across the waxy surface, releasing the sweet fragrance. The trunk of a hornbeam: muscled and sinewy, strong, I hold it. There is no end to what I feel. Sweetgum seedpods, poky; fern fronds, feathery; the dirt, crumbling. I grasp at everything.

It may seem I have evaded the simple question. In this disappearing world we have been conditioned, after all, to make our feelings disappear too. Always in the midst of ecological devastation, we are rarely if ever asked (throughout our years of school, at work, in the grocery store, driving down the highway, watching the news, or sitting in meetings) how the loss and wreckage make us feel, though we know we are in a pandemic of anxiety and depression. Sometimes, though, on an ordinary day when you are a writer, someone asks you to put your feelings into words. In describing this act of touching with my hands, I am feeling my way toward an answer.

Sixty-four thousand years ago, members of the *Homo* genus placed their palms flat on the walls of caves and blew the crushed powder of red ochre over them, creating stencils of their hands, the earliest human art. Our ancestors printed their hands this way onto rocks all over the world, for tens of thousands of years. I have not been to these caves but have looked at these images obsessively, the many hands overlapping, crowds of hands like layers of foliage, resonating with presence, vivid on the cave walls. Art is born of the impulse to see who we are, what our relationship to the cosmos is, and if these hands are our species' earliest artistic creations, I feel it's a worthy endeavor to keep looking at them, these hands that reach across time to wave at us, ghostly.

The stenciled hands are alongside drawings of deer, pigs, bison, horses, ibex, and aurochs. That is to say that one of the first endeavors of the uniquely human hand, the hand that creates art, was to reach for an understanding—the kind of *seeing* that art does—of the animals that our ancestors lived alongside, those whose lives fed and sustained theirs. The art-making hands depicted kinship, placed their hands among the animals.

We are familiar with a narrative that tells us it's the hand with its opposable thumb that makes us unique as a species, and by that it is meant superior. It has been said it's the hand that sets us above. But we are as unique as every other species and also created from long lines of other ancient beings; our opposable thumbs evolved in the great apes who lived before us, as they gripped and swung from tree branches in dense and fruitful canopies.

Human hands later rubbed sticks together, made fires, ground ochre, and created the paintings on cave walls. They sharpened stones, killed animals, skinned them, cooked meat over fires, pulled it off, handed the meat to others, fed their children.

Our ancestors made homes, sowed seeds, wove tapestries and blankets, and baskets for foraging, picked berries, cradled their infants, and healed one another with their hands. They clasped their hands together, folded them in front of them, raised them to the sky. They fluttered and waved them when singing, made, no doubt, shadow puppets behind leaping flames, their hands becoming birds. They grasped the world and their connection to it with their hands.

With their hands, the Haida and Tlingit people placed the first salmon they caught each winter upon an altar, writes Lewis Hyde in *The Gift: Imagination and the Erotic Life of Property*. They welcomed the salmon to the feast, told it how they wished a good journey upriver to all of its kind. A priest cut the salmon into small chunks and handed everyone present a piece of its flesh, sustenance that allowed them life. The priest carefully removed the intact skeleton of the salmon and returned it to the water—if this was not done, the salmon wouldn't know the people revered them and might not ply the currents upstream the next winter. All the bones of the year's catch, in fact, were given back to the river, hands tossing and dropping them into the currents.

The hands can have careful intention; they can act with reverence; they can give gifts to one another and give gifts back to the earth and its creatures. This is something the hands can do after they receive nourishment, after they take life and accept the gift of life. What the hands do is the story of our relationship to the world.

When industrialization came and the canneries were built at every river's mouth, millions of salmon were harvested without being touched by a human hand, the bones were not given back to the water, and the populations were depleted to nothing.

A story can be told about how the disappearance of the world around us corresponded with the replacement of the feeling human body with machines.

The Industrial Revolution mechanized handiwork. Mechanical innovations seemed to hold out the promise of mass-producing happiness. Workers' hands were cut off often in factories, as they rushed to operate machinery. Modern people used their hands less and less as simple household tasks became automated, and goods they would have made by hand could be bought at stores. As each decade passed, the hands touched more human-made things, less of the earth from which the "raw" materials for those things came. This happened very fast. Contracts and business deals were signed with swift motions, copies of papers passed across desks that ordered whole forests to be felled. The upper classes and those who owned capital touched less than others with their hands and consumed the most resources.

In agriculture, work like planting, tilling, and harvesting was mechanized, so that even farmers touched the soil less and less, instead pulling levers on tractors and combines. With the press of buttons, they began to spray chemicals by the millions of pounds. Many farmers today never touch a plant, never caress a leaf in the field, put their hand to the soil. And so, they feel it less.

Nature education for children, when it was taught, became a training in *Look, don't touch,* as if nature were behind a wall of glass, and we were only visitors to a museum. This bred and reinforced feelings of separation and isolation—of sadness. A nature we don't reach out and touch is one we don't belong to, are not a part of. Hands were told to stay still, to hold their pencils, to turn to page fifty-two of the textbook. Hyperactivity and attention deficit diagnoses were given to hordes of children of my generation, my young classmates and friends heavily medicated. I remember our fingers tapping the desks, our hands fidgeting and doodling. I watched my friends poke and pinch their neighbors, pull the hair of whoever sat in front of them. Stress balls and fidget toys became a thing for students and those who worked in offices alike, things you could purchase to keep the hands busy.

When I received my ecological education in college, I learned of the destruction our kind had done with our hands. It seemed we could only do violence, that our hands wielded too much power. I felt guilt, sorrow, shame, grief, anger, hopelessness. I wrung my hands. Anything we touched seemed doomed, and I was afraid to touch anything.

That flood of emotions has not subsided, and I don't imagine it will as long as I'm living. As an accompaniment, though—as a practice, as a way of moving through my feelings, of staying in my animal body—I try to feel with my hands.

I grasp at the long stalks of grass gone to seed in the field, the tops like woolly worms. And a woolly worm, scrunching itself in a rippling motion forward across the asphalt. Do you think I can help myself?—the foreign pleasure of its feet pricking my skin, each barb pulling away, miniscule yet pointed sensations on my arm. I feel a smile breaking across my face.

In the kitchen, I cup a fluttery moth, feel its determined and powdery wings beat against my palms. I release it into the night. My hands flap open under the scattered stars. When we touch the earth, we are *touched* by it, for the word also refers to some interior motion in us, some subtle transformation.

We have touched every place on the planet now, but as our species' reach has expanded, ironically, we touch the world less and less with our hands, and we've lost the feeling that we are being touched back. To touch is active, but to be touched is passive; it requires us to acknowledge the agency and power of what touches us.

I stare at the hands on the cave walls. They belonged to the first of our species who were touched by the world, moved to make art. The hands are buried deep in the earth, in the layers of the past—thus preserved, they are always reaching toward us, toward a future they would never touch. And yet they do touch us, with the red ochre dust they left. Did they ever imagine that the world that touched them would disappear?

Grasping my pen, making marks on the empty pages, I am one in their lineage, reaching toward answers for who we are, what our place in this story is. I see in their hands a flowering in the black universe, as each of our tiny fists opened like a blossom when we emerged from the womb and reached to feel the world: other hands, faces, the fur of animals, vines, insects, and everything and all of it.

The hand opens in kinship with life. I pull stones up through the riffles from the creek bed, smoothed by years of water's caress. Holding them, I feel less need to shop, to grab every newest and latest thing, to fidget. I feel at those moments that everything is a gift, and I am full of gratitude. A single stone can do that. I think we could feel our way forward like this, in the darkness, through the disappearances.

PART III

Love, Get Angry, and Love Some More

We have every right to feel anger at what has been and continues to be done to our world. Right now, there may be no more powerful act than to share that anger with those making decisions about our future. Anger—rooted in our love for the places, lives, and life we know.

Rage, Rage against the Dying

KATHLEEN DEAN MOORE

We live in the time of mass dying, we are told. I can confirm the dying part, just by looking off my deck at low tide. Most of the mottled sea stars and sun-stars have disappeared from Alaskan shorelines, due to a virus made more virulent by warming seas. I have watched as whole constellations of starfish dissolved. One after another, their arms broke off and crawled away. The humpback whales are hunting alone in shallow water now, rolling on their sides to suck up stray perch, rather than erupting gape-jawed through huge schools of herring. I've seen no evidence of young whales in the inlet, nor evidence of their dying; when they starve, they sink to the ocean floor, too thin to float. The Sitka spruce are stressed by hot, dry summers; the yellow cedar are stressed by winters without snow to keep their roots from freezing. All along the northwest Pacific coast only 5 percent of the past crowds of salmon return to the streams.

So. What is an appropriate emotional response to mass dying?

We should love a dying place, we are told, the same way that we love a dying person—a father or friend, say, or a mother. Nobody had to teach me how to love my mother as she choked on the fluids of diseased lungs. I knew that each moment with her was precious, each memory shared was a gift. All I wanted was to hold her forever, as she grew more and more beautiful under her fever-pinked cheeks and silver hair. But I wasn't there when she died—a terrible decision. Too busy, too far away, too afraid. My guilt and horror at her death have been an inescapable grief.

Just so, as the lives in this inlet diminish day by day, and snowfields vanish from the mountains, my neighbors and I love them more and more, treasuring each moment among the anemones and barnacles that still crowd the tidepools, breathing their salt and tang deep into our lungs. We send marine-radio messages to alert the town if an orca passes by, remembering the great rafts of orcas we used to see. Neighborhood gatherings turn into beery wakes, as we tell stories of the rainbow puffs of great pods of whales exhaling. As for the inlet, it becomes more beautiful every day of the feverishly advancing summer—the silver tide burned pink by the sun hard on the horizon—the water clearer than ever before because rain has not come to overflow the tannic muskegs. When turnstones arrive one by one, rather than in great piping, chuckling flocks, the grief we feel is mixed with dread, anticipating the final loss. We linger at the edge of the ebbing tide, wishing we could hold it in our arms forever, or we turn away, afraid.

This terrible sorrow is a good and necessary thing, we are told, a measure of the magnitude of the gifts we have lost. We must embrace our grief, sit with it, trust it.

Or so we are told, and it's probably true. But this also is true:

We live in the time of mass dying, only because we live in the time of mass killing. The Earth's life-sustaining ecosystems are not dying of "natural causes," whatever that means. They are being killed. No, not just *being* killed. People are killing them. Standing at whiteboards in corporate offices, men plan and execute ecocides cruel and dreadful. The methods of killing are overheating, poisoning, demolishing, burning, starving, mining out, bulldozing, and drowning—to name a few. The killings are not accidental; they are intentional and knowing, or lethally reckless. The killings are collateral damage in some cases (see, for example, *fracking*), in others, the point of the entire corporate enterprise (see *industrial-scale fishing*), and often both (see *logging*).

Industrial timber companies suffocate salmon in streams silted and overheated, by cutting to mud the ancient forests that would have shaded the streams. Industrial fishing fleets starve the whales or pin them in ghost nets, while the Navy deafens them and petroleum-chemical companies poison them. Indonesian palm oil corporations bulldoze jungles for new plantations, displacing the orangutans and elephants. While they drill and burn and bank massive profits, the executives of ExxonMobil connive to gut legislation that might stop them from overheating land and sea—succeeding, even in the very month that temperatures hit 115 degrees in Seattle and higher along the intertidal shores. The heat killed billions of mussels on the rocks and untold numbers of beings hiding among them—skeleton shrimp and shore crabs and baby leather stars and anemones the size of a fingernail and, honestly, no one knows what else. All steamed to death and rotting. Corporate decision-makers have already caused so much green-house gas to be released that the oceans are as overheated as if bombers had dropped three Nagasaki-magnitude bombs into the sea every second for the last thirty years. The oceans are not dying; men are killing them.

My mother didn't just die; I'm convinced that she was killed by executives of the Ford Motor Company, who found it cheaper to filter their toxic smoke through the lungs of distinguished old women than to pay for industrial filters. Children and young adults in oil-and gas-drenched fields are not so much dying of leukemia as they are poisoned by executives who, by injecting a potent mixture of toxins into aquifers, are conducting large-scale experiments on human subjects, in direct violation of the Nuremberg Principles. How ExxonMobil will kill my whistling grandson and the grand-daughter with the honey hair—with what particular form of toxic chemicals or heat-induced virus or hunger or storm—I do not know and seethe to imagine. But oh, how the uber-executives must chortle among themselves, to see how quickly we bereaved are giving in to grief at the dying, overlooking the methodical and hugely profitable killing they order every day.

These are not accidental killings or inadvertent harms. These are business plans, purposefully designed to maximize profits "I hope you didn't know," Greta Thunberg told the oil and gas executives. "Because if you knew and you didn't stop, I would have to call you evil." Of course, they knew. ExxonMobil has known since 1977 that their business plan would wreck the world. Forty years ago, they launched a scientific research program that warned of global climate catastrophe, even learning how much carbon dioxide could be absorbed by the oceans.

So. What is an appropriate emotional response to mass killing?

Fury.

Revenge.

Action. Name the evil. Name the profanity of the destruction, the sacrilege against creation. Name the sins against the children of all species. Name the injustice to the poor and voiceless, crying out from future times. Name the betrayal of the legacy of human intelligence and virtue. Name the cruelty, the suffering. Name the treachery of governments in collusion with the corporations. Courts have a long history of apportioning shared responsibility for wrongs both civil and criminal, and assigning penalties and punishments; unleash them to do their work.

Tear away the social license of corporations to profit and destroy. We are witness to crimes of cosmic dimensions. Unthinkable, that we would allow people to enrich themselves by destroying the ancient fecundity of the planet, the millions of years of evolution that created the whales, the starfish, the cedars, the very future of our children. It's a crime against time, inconceivably evil.

The executives will try to make us blame ourselves for buying and burning their products, even as they use every trick in the book—through advertisements, legislation, taxes, and lobbying—to bind us hand and foot to a fossil-fuel economy. But it is no longer enough to say, "This is wrong, and I will not participate." We have to say, "This is wrong, and I will not allow it." Clear water, nourishing neighborhoods, deep green forests, the lives, all the lives on Arctic plains and ocean currents, on savannahs, the children and their silver-haired grandmothers: it's wrong to destroy these for corporate profit. They are not for sale; they belong to the future of the everlasting Earth.

We will mourn. Of course we will. We will bury our faces in our hands and cry inconsolably or stare vacantly at the barren beach. So much is lost. So much shimmering beauty. We will cry for the lost wings and silenced songs, for sunstars that danced on twenty-four ballerina legs, for singing toddlers who cannot begin to imagine what has been taken from them. This grief is right and good. But we must sharpen our sorrow into action. We must burn our grief into rage.

Why I Write for Birds

J. Drew Lanham

Urgency is essential for wild things, big and small—airborne, sea-tossed, or tunneled underground. The featherweight warbler at midnight flying across a full moon, guided by stars and instinct. Passing over abysmal gulf and land expanses, that may or might not be, to land in a random tree. What tells it where to come down? The thousand-pound bison, Tatonka, wandering because it feels a compulsion to graze we can never know There is something out there that brings life and force together. Much we can see; some we can explain by science. Volumes are unknown to us. Cause and effect become guesses more than not. The mysteries between known and unknown feed our fascination. I am a witness to as much as my life will allow—here in my southern Piedmont home—or when allowed, far away. Wildness to me is inside as well as "out there." My unwillingness to relent to the control of convention. To be on the edges always of feelings, to break the boundaries of expectation.

My life lies at the intersection of three axes—identity, place, and nature—more specifically My Blackness, My Southern Rural-ness, My Love Affair with Wild Birds and Wild Places. My job (and desire) is to have people see those three things aren't unique to me, but perhaps undercounted, as valuable and viable. It's a complex and messy but necessary task to bring the three into a light that doesn't get swallowed up by a convenient, cleaner narrative—to not get whitewashed out or colored over. I do that by writing to it as beautifully and as forcefully as I can. I think that's activism to move an agenda forward in some way that creates a larger change behind the action than existed before it. Even if that change is a different thought process heaved up on some previously flat plain of some old paradigm. I want people to be changed after they read what I write. More aware. More thoughtful. More passionate. Angrier. Sadder. Happier. Whatever. Strike the hot hay in the noonday shining sun with an iron that's hotter'n hell. I want that. It's an immediacy that won't wait on proper protocol or even publication in the "right" journal.

How do I bring my urgency to the fore? I watch birds. I study birds. I absorb birds with a yearning many days of wanting to be one. But since I cannot be a bird, and knowing full well Icarus's ego-fallen fate, I write about birds. I write for birds. I write to birds.

I write in poem and prose. I word-craft in short form social media and long essay. I two-finger tap in minuscule mobile phone font and still sometimes scribble in longhand—an illegible chicken-scratched script that lie scattered in notepads and pieces of journals as draft stories and ragged verse. I gather it all and weave and wrap until there is some story in which I can nest.

I sit and watch and think about the beings I know intimately by song and plumage and habit. I write often with no intent of anyone else ever seeing, but as an exercise in solo worship and mind space sacrifice. A murmuration becomes a sudden meditation. A call from a plover, alms. There is this melding of realities that causes me to lose track of responsibility and time. It is a selfish act and small personal space that I do not always willingly share with other humans. That might be wrong-hearted, but it is who I have become, an introverted ornithologist codependent on this ornitherapy that the birds give without cost.

But I gladly pay anyway. Knowledge is power and the more I understand the interactions between earth, sky, bird, and us, the better armed I become to defend the soil and water on which we all depend. I pay with attention and time. I pay by becoming more familiar with birds than a cataloging of numbers seen will ever show. Yes, I know birds by chips and churs and self-harmonizing sonata. I know birds by the flash of red and gold epaulette. I know birds by miraculous journeys spanned across watery gulfs and landscape lain desolate by development. I know them by the way they launch themselves into the air on a faith absent worshiping any Gods except lift and thrust. I know them by home—by my native Piedmont fragmented into jigsaw pieces, Blue Ridge hanging on to what's left of wildness; by low country salt marsh pluff mud stinking so good of sulfur. I know them by places far away—the tundra swan winging through moonlight in the South Carolina Low Country going back to some Arctic realm; by the handful of less than an ounce of feathers surviving predator and destructive perversion to perch itself in my fortunate view—to grace my puny ground tethered existence here. I connect birds to past and present. I place my hope in them for future presence.

I see a bird. I watch that bird. I absorb that bird mostly without worrying how many other birds I might see or scribe on a list. That bird is the only bird until the next bird comes along. I take in the places—the forests and tangles and seacoasts and rolling prairies. I pay closest attention to a single bird's ways of being. Ascribing some name to it—red-winged blackbird, black phoebe, black-necked stilt, black vulture, black-and-white-warbler— most are relatively easy identification tasks for me now. I see myself some- how in each of them, can feel some of the same struggles—envy their ability to slip the ties that bind and find freedom in flight.

The difficulty in my watching is the ever-degrading context that makes the joy insular. I'm grieving loss and losing ground in the mourning. I watch from an island surrounded by a world that seems ever to be falling down in pieces around me. Birds are an escape sometimes, but ignoring that dim sea rising, no matter how grim, is the sin. And so, as I write to beauty I must wind daily, toxic streams of news that pass through my mental bin- ocular view. I must write to the violence, the news of wars and rumors of wars—of racial injustices, and hash-tagged movements. It is the socio- politically fragmented and climate-inflamed Anthropocene landscape over which we are all migrating and so cannot be ignored. To write about birds and not about their struggles would be akin to writing about Black people as if enslavement and Jim Crow and police brutality and mass incarceration never existed. That I have stake in two worlds that converge at my oneness is a best blessing and a worst curse. Both suffering and celebration fall to me. My Black life matters most to me, and I won't deny my own soul's well- being to make birds small and just something to be seen without deeper connection and feeling.

I write about birds because they are my last best hope for heaven's Angels here on earth—or whatever sublime unearthly things nirvana or Brigadoon or any alleged paradise I could ever pray for beyond the exis- tence I know, might hold. Beyond the fated disappointment of humans who fail in loving consistently—birds do not. I ask nothing of them, and they give everything. There is no morning song I wish ever the cardinal had undone or promise of inspiring or nest dream-weaving any wren has ever broken or fallen short of. The only possible way for birds to fail me is if they cease to be. For that reason alone, but countless others, I must work to make sure that such a thing does not happen.

A mantra for my bird-brained feather-adoration: Watch, revere, repeat. Watch, revere, repeat. Writing about birds; to birds; for birds—that is reverence. My identity falls in line with their plight. Their wildness in spaces from my South Carolina backyard to far-away corners of the world stitches them to me as fellow earth beings whose well-being or struggles signal how we should or should not be. The Golden Rule extends from our hearts to their wings. Watch, revere, repeat. That's the urgency of my writing work, to bring head and heart to some work of greater love—wild birds for me are conduit and key.

The Practice of Anger in a Warming World

Genevieve Guenther

Anger is a controversial emotion in moral philosophy. Both Plato and Aristotle connected anger with a desire for justice, but the Stoics—who carried the day in ancient Rome and enjoy ongoing life in the boardrooms of Silicon Valley—thought that the mark of a good man is his capacity never to lose his cool. Jesus, of course, recommended turning the other cheek, and Wrath was named one of the seven deadly sins by the medieval church. Even Hume, Hutchinson, Shaftesbury, and Smith—the eighteenth-century philosophers of sentiment who put emotions at the center of our moral life—tried to separate out "anger" from "righteous indignation," a sensation supposedly purified from any taint of the desire to hurt evildoers in revenge for their evil deeds. Modern America's most popular moral philosopher, Martha Nussbaum, makes largely the same move. And the popular culture of "self-care," which passes for ethics (or "spirituality") in our individualistic, neoliberal age, encourages us not to feel anger at all, directing us rather to "let it all go" and embrace gratitude rather than resentment or, god forbid, revolutionary fervor.

Feminist and Black thinkers are dismantling the shields that philosophers and yoga gurus have erected to protect the social world and its unjust systems from the anger of those it has harmed. Audre Lorde tells us that "Every woman has a well-stocked arsenal of anger potentially useful against those oppressions, personal and institutional, which brought that anger into being. Focused with precision it can become a powerful source of energy serving progress and change."* Implicit in this allegory of anger's power is the idea that anger is an involuntary response—something that arises instinctively when someone with self-respect is subject to a social slight (in this case the systemic "social slight" of misogyny). Women, Lorde suggests, feel their anger only to repress and hoard it away, but they should loosen that store of old rage on the world as a "powerful source of energy serving progress and change."

While I totally agree that anger is a galvanizing energy source that can fuel social movements, I don't actually think that activists, and climate activists in particular, should assume that anger is a purely involuntary sensation that we can choose to use productively only after we unwittingly experience it. I think that anger is a feeling that we can actively *cultivate* as a political and even spiritual practice. Not only can anger power the climate movement, energizing us to fight for our survival, it can also rescue us from that alluring, double-faced siren of nihilism and despair.

I will admit that nihilism and despair are very attractive—sexy, even, considering also they're the affects that all too easily signify "intellectual sophistication" in the Anthropocene. Embracing cynicism and hopelessness allows you both to look tough, as if you have the backbone to face devastating truths about global warming, but also to take yourself off the hook of the duty to work towards resolving the crisis. (You are not free from that duty just because the problem cannot be solved by you alone.) Yet this performative despair is not the only despair we need to avoid. We also need to guard ourselves against—or heal ourselves from—being rolled by the huge waves of fear and grief that can wash over you when you allow yourself to really see what is happening to our planetary life-support system. Flat out after being hit by one of these waves, trying to catch your breath, you can either stay down or you can try to regenerate your anger. I'm here to recommend the latter. Anger will give you the hot desire to stand up and dive back into the work of taking power away from the people maintaining the systems that are killing us.

I know this from experience. I began my career as an activist when the *New York Times* hired Bret Stephens, a *Wall Street Journal* columnist and an inveterate climate denier. Fueled entirely by righteous indignation—my sense

*Audre Lorde, "The Uses of Anger: Women Responding to Racism," Keynote Address, National Women's Studies Association Conference, Storrs, CT, June 1981.

of betrayal and outrage that the paper of record, my companion through the contemporary world, would promote climate denial—I wrote a petition calling for the *Times* to rescind Stephens's offer. And I wasn't the only one who was pissed: my petition got a lot of press and ended up with forty thousand signatures. Stephens stayed at the *Times*, of course, but the editor that hired him was fired a few years later for publishing an op-ed that argued the federal government should call in the military to control Black Lives Matter protesters. Perhaps we planted the seed of the idea that this editor was too inclined to publish political commentary that should have no place in a twenty-first century democracy? In any case, my outrage catapulted me into full-time activism, and I've never looked back.

And yet—and this is a big "and yet!"—there have been all too many moments when I've felt like I could not go on as a climate activist because the work was too painful. I've felt this way in late summer especially, after months of coping with the intensity of a new and oven-like New York City heat while witnessing the death and destruction that even just 1 degree Celsius of warming is raining down on our backs. I've felt this way after reading particularly dire scientific reports. And I've felt this way when I've thought about how much speculative negative emissions technology the Intergovernmental Panel on Climate Change (IPCC) has put into its decarbonization pathways. In these moments I sometimes want to throw up my hands and just live out my very privileged life doing some other kind of work.

But instead of indulging these wishes or trying to escape my feelings of despair (although of course sometimes I do that too—generally with whisky), I try to remember why I became concerned about the climate crisis in the first place: because I have a son whom I love very much and to whom I want to say when I die that I did everything I could to help halt global heating.

But here's the thing: my love for my son is actually not enough. Just as I spent some years studying climate science and climate communication by myself before I explicitly became an activist, I can feel my love for my son and for innocent people everywhere, and that love will make me care about the climate, but I can't *move* on that love, transmute it into action, without my anger. So, what I do is turn my attention away from the purely material world (what before climate change was known as "nature") and focus like a hawk on the people who are causing global heating. I literally sit down, as if I were going to meditate, and I close my eyes and take slow and deep breaths and really let myself *feel* the crackling electricity of fear and the sharp ache of grief in my body. I try to stay in this place until the visceral intensity fades. And once it fades I turn my attention to the people who have knowingly caused the climate crisis and who are currently preventing the decarbonization of the economy and who are quite literally putting the lives of billions of people in danger and who are destroying the only livable planet in the known universe so they can make a few years more of profit and then, guess what? I get furious all over again.

This fury helps me remember that climate change is an expression of the murderous violence being done to us—and especially to our children—by the people propping up the fossil-fuel system. In my rage and incredulity I somehow start to feel like I could not live with myself if I just shrugged and walked off and let them get away with it. And once more, I'm in the breech, my friends; I've stood up and run into the breech once more.

Let me be clear. Living like this is exhausting. Honestly, I would rather not have to cultivate my anger. But we're in an existential crisis and people fighting for their lives get tired. It's also important to remember that as an unwitting reaction to stress, or when it's directed towards innocent people, anger is destructive and dangerous. Cultivating anger should be part of an overall project of managing one's emotions to do the least harm and the most good possible. But I think the rage of the climate activist does do good. It seeks power, I believe, not to dominate and punish the people who are harming us, but simply to end their harms and prevent them from reoccurring. It seeks not retribution but restitution. It seeks justice. That is why cultivating anger is not just a political but spiritual practice: in seeking justice, it enables us to put our love into action. Indeed, it enables us to make our love for the world the very meaning of our lives. And if there is anything that can counter the death-dealing of the people running the fossil-fuel system, it is love. Let's do everything we can to bring that love into being.

The Dying Elm

Ken Hada

As on most homesteads in central Oklahoma prairies, cedar and sumac thrive here, redbud sprinkled among them, an occasional persimmon. Cottonwood, pecan, and post oak accent the pastures of native bluestem and wildflowers. But the dying elm will never leaf again. In early summer, it stands tall, upright, but leafless, while all other trees are green.

Standing in bald glory, it dominates my view, commands memory. It has been a favorite tree on these twenty-nine acres I am privileged to call home—my focal point as I sip coffee at sunrise, as I watch sunset through leafy branches. Even in starlight, it demands attention. It was always full of birds—a familiar stopping place for those passing through this major flyway, and for those that stay year-round. Now only a handful visit the bare branches.

I won't cut it down though. I will let this tree fall in its own time.

Cottonwoods, eighty feet tall, rise along the creek where fawns and does take cover. Rugged, handsome oak covers the western hillside of the property. This topography, known nostalgically as The Cross Timbers, once was covered with hardwoods, but in our zealotry of playing cowboy—from the mid-nineteenth century till today—we have gratuitously overgrazed, bulldozed, and ignored their ecological stability native to this place. For now, the Chuck-will's widow survives in their cover, singing through summer nights till sunrise.

Seven large pecans decorate the middle pasture, offering a sustainable feast for deer and crows, among others. Birds fill the limbs, with barred owls preferring the higher branches. Scissortail flycatchers, in the remaining prairie grass, helicopter between fence rows and the lower branches.

So why does this singular elm attract me? Obviously, its barrenness stands out, displays a presence by its absence—and that presence haunts. What took its life? Elms are susceptible to disease. Did three weeks of subzero temperatures this past February kill it? This part of the continent rarely endures such long bouts of unyielding cold. But no other trees died as a result of that frigid month, only the elm. Why?

I may learn the cause someday. For now, I choose to live with this mystery as a symbol for life—all life which is subject to sudden, unexplained death. In grief, we always feel the inexplicability of death. I want to hang on to mystery a while longer. I want to remember the elm in its lush, giving, greenness—hosting fifty birds at a time. I want to hold on to its past, and yes, my past too, even as I ponder and praise its graying decomposition.

There are other deaths too—but they are explainable. They are infuriating, victims of human ignorance, if not brutal stupidity. The Oklahoma dream is to have a gas or oil well, never mind the destruction of fracking, the littered skyline, the ruptured prairie. Never mind that the major energy companies routinely lay off employees in our ever-turning roulette of bust and boom. As I write, for miles along the highway, every tree within fifty feet of the shoulder is being destroyed to make possible a new four-foot shoulder and a few passing lanes, so we can drive even more recklessly, listening to talk radio telling us how to think. Trees forty-plus feet from the proposed shoulder, offering no danger or interference to traffic, are foolishly demolished.

The pastures, once filled with bluestem and native grasses, are being replaced with "improved" grasses, a holdover practice from the first days of homesteading that has led to soil erosion and loss of wildlife. The first order of business is to bulldoze the cedars, taking with them topsoil and well-rooted native grass, then bathe the substitute pastures with fertilizer and pesticides hoping for improvement overnight. We seem to have unlearned lessons from the Dust Bowl era.

Some poison coyotes, or chase them with automatic weapons (but they refuse to go away, which is why I love these ultimate survivors howling each night behind the hillside). Homes are not complete until thousands of dollars are spent to make a Victorian lawn, artificial as plastic. I still hear quail calling in summer, but unlike the coyotes, they must have native grasses for habitat. They will not survive subjugation of the prairies. We install costly

HDL yard lights, blot out the stars, blind the songbirds, and ruin human sleep. Little houses on the prairie ain't what they used to be.

These small prairie towns host a diverse population. A great variety of Native American peoples live here, many now mixed-blood, whose ancestors arrived after displacement from the southeast in the 1830s and other interrupted places in the north. I live within the Citizen Pottawatomie Nation, a people who arrived here in 1870, after several brutal removals from the Great Lakes. The Native tribes build empires based on casino income. I applaud their ironic sovereignty, do not envy their tribal wealth, admire their social progress that distributes services to tribal members. But even tribal institutions can be caught up in the phony frenzy misnamed "progress."

Most Black citizens seem relegated to the "bad" parts of these prairie towns. But even in this reddest of states, the social concerns of our country are ours too. One of the most memorable days of my life was marching in a Black Lives Matter rally in small-town Oklahoma, bravely organized by young citizens, while pickups lined the parade route loaded with neighbors, some, I'm sure, praying for a chance to shoot.

Oklahoma has always been diverse. Once there were more Black people in the "Territory" than Native Americans. Thankfully, there is steady cooperation among us most of the time. But when politics turns more irrational than football, and Jesus is reimaged as a marine, things can become heated. So, you vote for Kamala and divert your eyes from the Trump flags still flying—and the rebel flags that have never gone away.

What does this sociology have to do with ecology? Those flag-waving, gun-toting brethren, peaceful as long as they perceive they are in power, too often exhibit the same mind toward the environment as toward people. But I think, deep down, we all know that the earth and its inhabitants are eternally, concomitantly linked. Care for one begets honest care for the Other. A mutual respect for our diversity also involves protecting the water we all drink and the air that fills our lungs. Exploitation takes many forms. Indifference festers into hatred and then to self-destructiveness, where we live only for the moment in air-conditioned caves, our pampered lawns overtaking the prairies, ignoring the stars, unconcerned with anyone else.

I could keep quiet, look the other way. I'm white enough not to be bothered. I could just offer up prayers and sit on my hands and wait for the apocalypse.

But I can't because I'm aware. This is the paradox I live with. I suffer an abiding sense of loss because I am aware, but without awareness, nothing sustainable occurs. Too many fellow citizens refuse to notice the obvious disintegration of people and place. We sing with Rogers and Hammerstein: *We know we belong to the land / and the land we belong to is grand,* but that chorus sounds hollow when unexamined decay is assumed to be natural, or is cynically dismissed as one day closer to the end times. The love of landscape, which most Oklahomans openly claim, could be a common denominator for sustainability. Our shared sense of place should bind us together in honest stewardship, regardless of political preference. In too many cases, however, we have yet to emotionally accept the fact that we cannot have *some* of the benefits of nature without protecting *all* of nature.

In the meantime, we fill our credit cards trying to play like the privileged—on a lake with a bass boat and a seventy-horse motor, a high-powered rifle and a four-wheel drive "mule" for deer hunting, or an RV camp full of generators running satellite TV all night, drowning out the rapids of a stream, while tree frogs and owls call in vain throughout the night.

This state has recently leaned hard to the right politically, yet several hundred thousand of us have a different perspective. We align ourselves with Will Rogers, Woody Guthrie, Ralph Ellison, Clara Luper, James Garner, and so many other outliers who loved Oklahoma while refusing to be socially oppressive. We are scattered across this geographical space, even as we are scattered emotionally. We love our land; we respect our neighbors, know they are capable of great good. But we feel something is passing. We know the buzzwords: *Interdependence, Sustainability, Stewardship, Solastalgia, New Green Deal, Deep Ecology, Gaia, Mother Earth*—on and on. But knowledge alone won't save us. We need emotional conviction in our souls and courageous effort to fundamentally change. This, perhaps more than anything, marks the sadness I feel. The inability to convince others to make significant change seems insurmountable. We consume ourselves, and though social problems of race and gender equality always matter, if we don't establish a healthy, shared destiny as organic, mortal mammals, everything else finally disappears.

I celebrate the native goodness within this state, its diverse topographies and population. But I also hear the symphony of loss echoing through the hills. I fear its crescendo. So, I will not cut down this elm. Its death is a good death, unlike other manufactured destruction so thoughtlessly permitted. The dead elm has become a sacred tree.

A New Word to Describe New Feelings

Susan Clayton

I became interested in the psychology of environmental issues because of the emotions I heard when people talked about the natural environment. It started with their descriptions of pride in their home territory and love for specific trees. As I, and other people, focused more on current environmental crises, a wide range of negative emotions became apparent (in my own reactions as well as those of others). Fear and anxiety, yes. Sadness and grief. Guilt and anger. But positive emotions remained as well: pride, appreciation, and let's not forget hope, the emotion at the bottom of Pandora's box.

As a psychologist, I'm intrigued by the ways in which people respond to environmental topics. I'm even, though this feels a little inappropriate, excited by the fact that my work in conservation psychology is more relevant than it has ever been. These emotions, however, coexist against a backdrop of my own anxiety, fear, and grief, emotions that I am usually able to tamp down but that occasionally take me off guard and set my heart pounding. My experience is consistent with the emotions that I have seen among climate scientists: they, too, report feeling sad, angry, afraid; hopeful and optimistic; and excited by the opportunity to investigate the issue and the chance to do research that would really matter.

Emotions are fascinating and complex. They're both personal and communicative; genuine experience and performance. Although the feelings are real, we can talk ourselves into or out of experiencing many of them and even be unaware of our own emotional state. And this matters because they're contagious. If I feel fear, and express that fear, people around me are likely to feel at least a bit uneasy—to look around for a threat. If I talk myself out of that fear and express only calm or boredom, the people around me will take that as a signal that there is nothing to fear. This social communication that there is nothing to fear probably plays a big part in our collectively muted response to climate change. Some people who might be inclined to worry look around and see that most people are ignoring the issue, acting as if it's not a big deal. Since we only see what they communicate, we don't know that, in fact, many of them are scared and anxious. The observable response suggests that society is not concerned.

So, the way we talk about emotions is significant. The emotion experienced in response to environmental change isn't the end of the process but a part of an ongoing system: learning about a threat to nature, having an initial reaction, maybe discussing it with others or hearing about how others have responded, maybe modifying the initial emotional reaction, determining a behavioral reaction (including inaction), maybe doing something that modifies the threat, interpreting our own behavior, interpreting the behavior of others. . . .

And because the way we talk about emotions has an impact on our own experience of those emotions, the language we use matters. *Solastalgia* is a relatively new term that was coined to describe a feeling of sadness or loss associated with environmental change. It reflects a sense that an environment that used to give pleasure, security, or solace has changed and can no longer provide that solace. Solastalgia can be linked to a specific place, such as a former home or a location that was significant in childhood, but it can also result from perceived changes to a broader environment, such as "the mountains," "the Northwest," or even the entire environment. The feeling came before the word, but the word allowed a lot of us to recognize what we were feeling and so maybe feel it more strongly.

There exists, at least in Western society, a tendency to underappreciate and ignore the environment in which we find ourselves—something that has been called "environmental numbness." We may be unaware of how important it might feel for us personally to have a view of the sea or of mountains. I would have felt frivolous, for example, if I had made important life decisions, like where to go to college or where to work, based on the local environment. But I know how much I could be soothed simply by seeing a specific familiar pine tree, and how sad I felt when highway improvements destroyed the bank of sweetheart roses I used to walk past.

Having words that describe our emotional attachment to the natural world allows us to recognize that attachment, and to include it in the repertoire of ways in which we understand and experience nature. And it allows us to talk about these experiences to others.

Some of my research has involved observing zoo visitors—"watching people watching the animals" as one of those visitors described it when I explained what I was doing. Although people are no more saintly in a zoo than they are anywhere else, it was not uncommon for people to be carried away with their response to the animal. It wasn't enough for them to stand in silent appreciation; they had to try to convey their emotion to others. "I love him!" "He's awesome!" or even "Cool!" were not infrequent comments as people tried to put their appreciation into words. The results of my research were equivocal about the extent to which this motivated actual conservation behavior, but nevertheless it made me optimistic to see people express such positive emotion simply by observing animals—when from a strictly rational perspective there was no benefit to be gained from these interactions. People respond to animals. That reflects well upon human nature.

I feel something similar when I read about the emotional responses to climate change and environmental degradation. I wouldn't wish these experiences of environmental loss on anyone. But I have to admit that I'm heartened by the fact that people acknowledge a range of powerful emotions in response to environmental change; after all, this means that they are recognizing the personal importance of those changes.

To feel solastalgia is to remember the solace that preceded it. To grieve for environmental damage is to acknowledge the value that the environment has. And if we don't only feel it, but also talk about it, we can help others to acknowledge it and encourage society to acknowledge it. And maybe then our emotions, and our words for those emotions, can lead to changes.

Affirming Abundance

PRISCILLA SOLIS YBARRA

I am a queer, Chicana/x, US-based academic with the rare privilege of spending most of my life in one place. I live on the unceded lands of the Wichita and Caddo Affiliated Tribes, in an area known-for-now as North Texas. I observe vibrant spring and fall migrations of birds and butterflies; I watch the post oaks go through their cycles of bright to deep green, brown, and then bare limbs; I float my kayak on the various tributaries to the Arkikosa (Trinity) River; I watch cactus fruit ripen into delicious magenta; and I listen to the excited yips of coyotes at night. In this essay, I reflect on my budding practice of birding to help me to think through ways to mediate solastalgia.

About three years ago, I started paying more attention to my backyard birds. They themselves insisted I take notice. I saw the owl on July 24—I know because I took a photo of him, but I didn't bother to look up his name or other characteristics—song, habitat, frequency in my area. But that sighting tripped something in me. I started wondering about the other birds I regularly saw in my yard, and I learned their names—Carolina chickadee, tufted titmouse—in addition to the few I knew already from childhood—cardinal, mockingbird, blue jay, robin, vulture, crow.

My knowledge started expanding. Who is that little brown bird with the longish curved beak and the loud twitter? Carolina wren. And, hey, there's a woodpecker, except for—wait, there's another one that looks completely different!—red-bellied woodpecker and downy woodpecker. So, when a pair of black-throated green warblers—small yellow-and-white birds with the male sporting deep black feathers on his throat—showed up in my backyard in the fall, I had a little more of a clue about how special that was. Their return the following spring thrilled me. I was hooked.

I dedicate my writing and teaching to documenting the connection between my Mexican American culture, the land, and social justice. As such, one might think that my longevity of place would be reflected in my knowledge of its natural history—the local flora, fauna, and geology. But this awareness took hold only when I started bird-watching. And even then, I did not identify myself as someone who had the capacity to become a birder or a natural historian. I simply found in birding a comfort, a way to escape the constantly ticking clock, the urgency of linear time. I learned to dwell in place and with the cycles of seasonal being, to pay attention to the world in the ways my Mexican mother has been patiently suggesting for my whole life. I offer you the practice of birding as a strategy to mediate solastalgia, but I contextualize its practice within the intertwined histories of colonization and capitalism.

The way that birding helps me escape from linear time can connect me to Indigenous practices, if I let it. As Potawatami philosopher Kyle Whyte advises, linearity is only one way of experiencing time. He shares that Indigenous time centers on spirals: cycles, seasons, and relationships. A clan can draw its identity from the role they play during a seasonal event, say the time of wild rice cultivation, rather than from the accumulation of material goods or the longevity of power. This is a system of governance known as the "seasonal round system." Another way that spiral time can impact lived experience has to do with the maintenance of kinship ties among humans as well as between humans and other beings. Community members measure quality of relations by the maintenance of just reciprocities and mutual respect. My practice of daily birding gives me an opportunity to briefly inhabit spiral time, where I experience my friendship with the migrating birds, appreciate their appearance according to their own terms and needs, and do what I can to support their movements, such as setting out sugar water for the ruby-throated and black-chinned hummingbirds.

But what happens if I let myself follow the path of Whyte's argument about spiral time and consider bigger ways that understanding of time can mediate solastalgia? Whyte explains that when it comes to climate catastrophe, Indigenous peoples also inhabit a different timeline than the West. The Indigenous dystopia has already been taking place for over 500 years, and the Western present is the fantasy future of a settler colonial past. The

West's fantasy is coming to an end with its awareness of climate change and all of its accompanying losses, a phenomenon it labels the Anthropocene. An increasing awareness of these losses is what brings about feelings of solastalgia. However, colonized cultures have long suffered the consequences of the loss of our relations, human and beyond.

Canadian scholar Audra Mitchell argues that the present-day focus on species extinctions distracts from the ways that Indigenous people's relations with other beings have been deeply disrupted by colonization's violent displacements. She explains that colonization has already enacted a centuries-long mass extinction event by displacing Native nations from ancestral lands. Birding and natural history tell us that species are starting to go extinct at alarming rates, but that relates only to a Western timeline. The light of the relations that kept those species alive dimmed a long time ago.

Comparing Western linear time versus Indigenous spiral time cautions me that natural history tells a story too narrowly defined by the power dynamics of colonization and capitalism. I want to distance my observation of species, seasonal shifts, and local geology from a practice of science that accords to a Western imaginary and reinforces the same Enlightenment-era logics behind colonization and capitalism. I want to see how my experiences with the birds and the wind and the rain and the lizards and the frogs and the rivers do something else. I work toward rituals that reinstate ethical practices of respecting all of my relations, in a way that is consistent with my Indigenous kin. The practice I seek to establish resonates with what Potawatomi scientist and writer Robin Wall Kimmerer calls on us all to recognize when she explains how in her people's language of Potawatomi, "There is no it for nature. Living beings are referred to as subjects, never as objects, and personhood is extended to all who breathe and some who don't. I greet the silent boulder people with the same respect as I do the talkative chickadees."

What do we learn once we decide to turn toward the lessons that colonized cultures can offer from inhabiting a changed world for over five hundred years? First, we must take an honest look at the trauma bound up in that history. Modern Western cultures enslaved Black and Brown bodies in order to take over their lands and in pursuit of material goods such as gold, sugarcane, and cotton. All of these pursuits put Black and Brown bodies into antagonistic relation with the outdoors—learning to live in unfamiliar places, working inside caverns blown into the Earth, laboring under the hot sun for long hours. The descendants of the enslavers and colonizers still use Black and Brown bodies to mediate the downside of capitalist pursuits, to shield Western cultures from their own greed. Climate change and the ongoing extinction of species are now beginning to capture the attention of Western cultures. Black and Brown bodies cannot continue to mediate for the elites the consequences wrought by colonization and capitalism.

Yet, despite colonized communities' externally imposed proximity to some of the toughest aspects of survival, we continue our rich articulation of relations with all beings. My father planted a garden even though he grew up barely surviving on a Mexican American's farmworker wages during the Great Depression; my mother taught me herbal remedies even though her Brown skin and the traditional ecological knowledge connected to it were scorned when she immigrated to the US from México.

What emerges for me is a portrait of colonized cultures who insist on connecting with all of Earth's entities, even through the difficulties of colonization. I understand this as an affirmation of abundance that goes beyond the counting and categorizations of natural history. Yes, natural history tells a grim story today—with the numbers of birds dwindling at a rapid rate as just one example. But our ancestors' practices of affirming abundance and adapting our cultures to ongoing losses also tell a story of surviving and thriving—even when under assault. Anishinaabe scholar Gerald Vizenor calls this "survivance." Our ancestors and elders tell us a story of survivance. In this story, contemporary cultures can find ways to mediate solastalgia. But above all, we can hear a call to ally together against the destructive systems of colonization and capitalism.

This collection of essays on the topic of solastalgia prompts me to tell the story of my personal transformation into someone who started paying deeper attention to the place and beings of where I dwell, and how that practice of attention becomes a way to not only encounter solastalgia but also to confront colonization and capitalism. What I embrace is not an identity as a natural historian, environmentalist, or outdoor enthusiast but as an abolitionist. I celebrate the varieties of life and being that my culture and other colonized cultures have cultivated in the face of colonial violence. This is all the more reason to pay attention to the communities who resist colonization and commodification, to learn from the ways we affirm abundance, reject scarcity, and call for abolition. We have been developing ways to encounter the ongoing consequences of colonization, capitalism, and their attendant psychological and emotional difficulties for centuries, and now it is time for others to start paying attention to the lessons we can offer—not just to mediate the consequences but to remake the world.

Soliphilia in Beaverland

Ben Goldfarb

In the northeast corner of Washington State, not far from the Idaho border, runs Thompson Creek. The stream rolls off the southern flank of Quartz Mountain, traipses through pine and Douglas fir forest, and spills into a eutrophic sump called Newman Lake. Along the way it suffers just about every indignity a stream can suffer. Thompson Creek has been ditched and dredged, incised and channelized, eroded and straightened. Its floodplain has been mown and overgrazed and overrun with invasive grass. Today its lower reach is essentially a canal for the conveyance of phosphorus and sediment, a polluted payload that clots Newman Lake with oozy algal mats each summer.

Sometime during the nineteenth century, Thompson Creek experienced another, subtler abuse: it was robbed of its beavers. Before European arrival, as many as 400 million beavers frolicked in North America's waterways. The dams constructed by these paddle-tailed legions altered the very face of the continent. By my back-of-the-envelope math, beaver ponds historically impounded enough water to submerge a landmass the size of Nevada and Arizona put together. When white fur trappers systematically eradicated *Castor canadensis,* they destroyed this liquid landscape. Without beaver dams slowing flows and shunting water onto floodplains, streams eroded to bedrock and damp meadows desiccated. Fur-trapping was a seminal ecological catastrophe, as disastrous in its own right as logging, mining, or roadbuilding.

Thus it was long past time to bring beavers back to Thompson Creek—or, failing the animals themselves, a facsimile of them.

I drove out to Thompson Creek one fall afternoon to see the rebeavering in action and to take part myself. Low, gauzy clouds clung to the Selkirk foothills, flecked with golden larch and aspen. The stream, cut deep in a lank mat of reed canary grass, was so narrow I could've broad jumped the channel. It was a sad and diminished watercourse, as straight and simple as a cast fly line.

While Thompson Creek was bereft of meanders, it did not lack for hope. At several junctures, lines of head-high wooden posts cut across the stream, perpendicular to the flow, like the frames of picket fences. These were nascent Beaver Dam Analogues, or BDAs, and, with luck, they would be Thompson Creek's salvation.

BDAs are beaver-inspired structures that, while not quite as ingenious as the handiwork of the genuine rodent, share some of their ecological benefits. By slowing and spreading water, BDAs enhance stream complexity, build habitat, filter out pollution, and hydrate soils. They have become the American West's most fashionable stream-restoration technique, deployed to accomplish a broad litany of environmental goals. In Nevada, BDAs have fostered wet meadows for sage grouse. In Oregon, they've bolstered steelhead populations. In Montana, they're remediating the heavy metals churned out by mining operations. Not incidental to their appeal is their cheapness: While other restoration strategies require backhoes and front-loaders, BDAs call for little more than a hand-held post-pounder and volunteer labor. And, most crucially, they lay the groundwork for the return of beavers themselves, who ideally maintain the site in perpetuity—no contracts or permits necessary.

On Thompson Creek, the new BDAs were primarily intended to capture some of the stream's phosphorus load. The initial post-pounding had been performed by Kat Hall, the cheerful restoration director for a local group called the Lands Council, acting in partnership with the usual ecosystem of government agencies, nonprofits, academics, and landowners. Hall and a few conspirators had driven 400 wooden poles into the streambed, enough for eighteen BDAs, adhering to a design prepared by a Gonzaga University engineering team. Now the time had come to thread dozens of ponderosa pine saplings—recently harvested from a nearby park to reduce its fire risk—through the posts, forming a dense wall of boughs and needles that would impound water and inundate the floodplain, as an authentic beaver dam would. The rodent's role would be played by a gaggle of Gonzaga undergraduates, who shuffled their feet uncertainly in the damp grass. "After today, you'll be able to tell your parents that you got a credit for underwater basket weaving," Hall said, to a few nervous chuckles.

Hall gave them a quick tutorial in the art of dam construction, showing them how to sew the saplings through the posts and stomp them into place, a set of moves she called the "BDA dance." Those minimal instructions issued, she turned the students loose. Some donned waders or hip boots and plunged into the stream; others hauled pine boughs to the water's edge. They began to wedge the saplings into position, first tentatively, then with more abandon, grabbing the posts and swinging themselves around like gymnasts on parallel bars. Pine needles flew; mud splattered jeans and hoodies. "You want it to be a little bit random, a little bit messy," Hall called from the sidelines.

I slipped into the stream, grabbed a few branches myself, and jammed the butt-ends into the bank. Soon the BDA had solidified and a waist-deep pool had formed upstream. This was, I confess, immensely satisfying. The activity soothed the innate desire, shared by humans and beavers, to modify the trajectory of water. I recalled the half-flooded sandboxes in which I'd wallowed in my youth, digging channels and ditches and watching dirty trickles bend to my will. The students, too, seemed young and light; they laughed and teased and jousted with their saplings.

"You're gonna concuss me with that branch, Abby!"

"They really shouldn't have put the person with the worst spatial awareness in the stream."

"Stomping brush is how I'm getting rid of midterm stress."

"You guys are *way* too enthusiastic about doing the BDA dance."

Spend enough time in the company of beaver-lovers—Beaver Believers, we call ourselves—and you'll eventually notice a pervasive, ambient solastalgia. Beaver Believers tend to feel homesick for a home they've never known: a home dimpled by hundreds of millions of beaver ponds; a home webbed by braided and sinuous streams; a home that once flashed with salmon fry and vibrated with the chirrup of frogs. A lush blue wet green puddled home—a home whose architects were semiaquatic rodents, not short-sighted hominids.

Solastalgia, however, has an antidote, also coined by Glenn Albrecht: *soliphilia*, the deep affinity we feel for our beloved home places, and our sense of responsibility for their protection. Soliphilia is, I think, the emotion that animates stream restoration—a scientific discipline, yes, but also a value-driven one, a field that recognizes the inextricable connections between healthy watersheds and our own survival, and our moral obligation to repair the world we've broken. If solastalgia is, per Albrecht, a "negative" earth emotion, then soliphilia is a profoundly positive one, a sentiment born of love and joy. And, at risk of imputing my own feelings onto a passel of undergraduates, it was that love and joy I saw at Thompson Creek: the soliphilic pleasure of restoring one damaged corner of this shattered planet.

As Thompson Creek rose around me, I tried to visualize its trajectory. I imagined the BDAs forcing the creek onto its floodplain, the stream's old abandoned channels thirstily accepting this gift of water. A drastically simplified stream would become braided once more, irrigating a riparian area of glorious fecundity and complexity. Dry soils would rehydrate; willows would sprout. And on some future evening, a beaver would arrive of her own volition, swimming up from the lake or down from the headwaters. In gathering dusk, she would haul her bulk onto the bank, nibble a stem, and prepare to settle in the home that a few humans once remade for her, feeling, perhaps, some soliphilia of her own.

PART IV

Bring New Life into
a Disappearing World

If we parent now, what do we teach and tell our children about the world?
And whether we parent or not, how do we help to revive the world's life?

Wild Lessons from Poisoned Water

Douglas Haynes

In midsummer, Starkweather Creek is green and fringed with foam. The stagnant water reeks of rot. Nevertheless, I canoe up the straight channel draining much of Madison, Wisconsin's East Side with my four-year-old daughter, Iris. She laughs at the ropes of matted algae I pull up on my paddle and calls them "Yuck!" She marvels when a green heron startles like a dart from the dense reed canary grass along the shore. Her eyes scan the surface for the pinheads of painted turtles.

Since my family moved to a house near the creek in 2012, the scrap of marsh and woods around the waterway have helped us warm to our new neighborhood. The cackles of kingfishers and bugles of sandhill cranes echo over the creek. Muskrats rudder the water. Tooth-marked stumps left by beavers often dot the banks.

People of all ages and colors delight in the creek, too. When the water freezes, cross-country skiers blaze trails through the snow blanketing the ice. The rest of the year, kids and teenagers cast for bluegills and bass under a railroad bridge. One April, I saw a musky more than two feet long swimming upstream there to spawn.

All this life seems miraculous given Starkweather's history. It's a survivor. In the nineteenth and early twentieth centuries, the once meandering creek was channelized while nearly 4,000 acres of wetlands feeding the waterway were mostly drained. The creek swelled with sewage and effluent from the nearby United States Sugar Company. Since then, the sewage has been replaced by runoff from the streets, parking lots, highways, shopping centers, and the airport that have covered most of the creek's twenty-four square mile watershed. On a map, the waterway's branches look like a child's Etch A Sketch of randomly connected straight lines.

Now, the Madison airport and its Air National Guard base pose a new problem. A few months after our summer paddle up Starkweather, ominous signs appear along the creek warning that it is contaminated with PFAS, a group of so-called forever chemicals used for decades in certain kinds of firefighting foams, nonstick pans, and waterproof jackets. At the same time, the Wisconsin Department of Natural Resources announces new fish consumption guidelines for Starkweather Creek and the lake it feeds—Lake Monona—due to exceptionally high levels of one PFAS chemical, PFOS (perfluro octanesulfonate). PFOS accumulates in the human body for years and is linked to developmental impairments in children, altered hormone regulation, and higher cancer risk, among other health threats. The new guidelines restrict consumption of all but the smallest fish from these waters to one meal a month. The health threat of PFOS disproportionately impacts low-income Madison residents who depend on Lake Monona for a source of food.

The primary source of contamination is the firefighting foam used by the Wisconsin Air National Guard's 115th Fighter Wing at the airport. The foam has been sprayed there since the late 1970s at least, according to government reports cited in *The Wisconsin State Journal*. Despite this foam's public health dangers, the Air National Guard hasn't complied with the Department of Natural Resources' call for a prompt cleanup.

Starkweather Creek makes this country's priorities clear. The Air National Guard can ignore its responsibility while parents must explain to their children that the creek where they learn to paddle and fish is poisoned. No one knows what the spiritual consequences of this dissonance are, nor what the physical harms may be to people who live near the creek. We all pay an unquantifiable price for the F-16 jets that rattle our house walls and force my children to cover their ears. What words can make sense for my two daughters that their beloved creek has been polluted so we can have ear-splitting jets nearby? How do I hide my panic when they inevitably fall into the water when feeding ducks or skipping rocks?

Growing up male in the American Midwest, I learned that showing emotional vulnerability is a sign of weakness. Now I must accept that the Earth is as vulnerable as I am. I feel like a boy glimpsing his father crying for the first time. There's no way to look at the father, the Earth, or the future the same way again. Not only does this vulnerability seem unspeakable, but I'm left bereft of the words to speak it.

Going to the creek with my daughters now fills me with a fear both ineffable and ever-present. The same gut-churning fear I feel whenever I admit to myself the secrets I keep from my daughters about how humans are unraveling our biosphere: climate crisis, mass extinction, plastic and endocrine disrupters permeating the world's waterways. For me, the creek represents the way our diminishment of the wild world is both seen and unseen, public and intensely private. We talk about it in the news but rarely in person.

Around the same time the signs warning about PFAS appear by the creek, hundreds of Canada geese gather there. I take Iris to see them. When the birds thunder into the air together, she shouts, "The geese are shaking the sky!" Her joy reminds me that even a poisoned little wild place can still connect us with the diversity of life. And the persistence of this diversity awes me every day on my walks by the creek. Maybe doggedly finding and celebrating that surviving variety of life in unexpected places can provide a well of courage to confront the vulnerability of the Earth we've created. Enough to at least grant us words for what persists rather than just what's missing.

The winter begins unusually warm, and the creek remains open into January. Then in a cold snap, the water freezes overnight, fashioning a clear, clean sheet of ice. The geese are gone, but the unvarnished elements offer a different kind of beauty. I stop on a footbridge over the creek and brush a heap of snow from the railing. The snowflakes shimmer in the low, fading sunlight. A breath of wind spreads the snow into a sparkling tail that dusts the ice like sugar, sweetening for an instant my knowledge of what taints the water beneath.

Mourning Songs Are Love Songs

Leah Naomi Green

I picked black raspberries for Glen when he was dying of cancer on a cot in his living room. I discovered the patch under the power line at the bottom of the road to our houses. Or—as so many have done, entering a lived-in land—I thought I had discovered it.

Black raspberries are my favorite. They are small and always sweeter than I remember. They are also a staple in our freezing and canning for the year—skills we learned largely from Glen and his wife Peggy, who, as it turns out, had been harvesting from that patch since before I was born. The two of them taught me most of what I know about growing food, heating with wood, needing and therefore attending to the place where I live. In fact, our young family now lives in the house that Glen built by hand—I am looking right now at the floorboards where that hospice cot stood.

At the beginning of the pandemic, the black raspberries were ripening, small and green in the centers of their flowers. I was driving the gravel road to our house with my daughters in the back seat and had to stop the car when I saw it gone: the whole patch cleared, the power company truck, blinding white in the right of way.

I fell into an instinctive mourning there in the car. My daughters picked up on it quickly. *This is how to mourn* it seemed I was saying; they were learning and reflecting the lesson in real-time. And, in truth, it felt like a sacred responsibility to model it: *this is loss. This is how to make room for feeling loss.* By the time we were up the hill to our house we were, all three, holding full-on vigil.

My daughters told their father about the black raspberries as he helped unbuckle them from the car seats, their speech and eyes low, like mine. But his voice lifted. "They'll regrow," he said. "That patch grew there because of the clearing for the power line." He told them that, had it not been for the power company, that spot would be as wooded as the rest of the mountain and much too shaded for a berry patch. In a few years, he pointed out, because the patch had been cleared, we would have black raspberries again—or something else.

Ben and I met at a Buddhist monastery in the dead of winter. He was processing the end of a marriage and the dissolution of his Christian faith. I had just finished my graduate work and, guarding my own heartbreaks with a borderline eating disorder, was on my way to Virginia where I knew that Glen and Peggy were homesteading and growing food, having raised three boys. I knew that I wanted to live richly without depending much on money, and Glen and Peggy had proven to me that such a life was possible. I did not yet know how to grow that life. Certainly, neither Ben nor I knew that it was the very disruption and decomposition of our previous worlds (relationship, faith, control, self-image) that would make the growing conditions right.

This kind of compost/growth imagery is basic to the Plum Village tradition of Buddhism in which Ben and I met. It's a tradition that continues to be central in our marriage and life. "No mud no lotus" says its founder, Zen Master Thich Nhat Hanh. His is an understanding of reality based on continual transformation rather than on concepts of life and death.

It's an understanding illustrated by ecology. Death is not escapable—neither experiencing it nor causing it. It is a biologically requisite stage in the life cycle. Without death, we have no soil, no "mud," no "fund of things," as Wendell Berry has called it, from which new life comes. I know this. I see this everywhere on our homestead, and it's a favorite theme of the poets I love most. So why do I still mourn the loss of the black raspberry patch? And why do I feel it is my responsibility as a parent and a human—who *can* feel mourning, who does feel complicit in violence—to do so?

Death may be a necessary stage of life, but destruction—that is, more death than is helpful to life, or death from which life will take a long time to emerge (for example, the excess extraction and release of carbon)—destruction is worth the hard work of resisting and training ourselves away from.

The black raspberry patch will grow back, but it will not grow back as it was. And though the earth is in no anthropogenic danger of "dying," it is in the process of anthropogenic changes, which will make life difficult for many species, including humans, and impossible for some. It will not grow back as it was. This may not be the kind of "end point" often imagined as *death*, but from the perspective of a human lifespan it is great *loss*. And it requires mourning. That is, it requires me to take good care of my sadness or hurt or guilt or fear, to attend to them lovingly, to try to offer—as I would through the loss of a person I love and depend on—ways to say *thank you*, and *I'm sorry*, and *what can I do to help*?

I mourn the wood thrush, even while I hear it sing. Or, not the wood thrush, but the thought of the woods without its song, and the thought of my children's lives without its song. Without that song, my life would be poorer. But does that mean my children's lives will be? What is sacred to me is so sacred to me. And because I am human I will mourn when those sacred things pass. I will mourn them because I love them. I *do* want to model this mourning for my children—I want to show them that grief is made out of love. Mourning songs are love songs and, in singing them, I can sing back to the wood thrush *I love you, I love you, I love you*. I want to teach my children how to feel sacredness and love and therefore mourning, but I don't want to insist they feel those things about the same berries and birds that I do. Once, there were no black raspberries where I live and no place for them to grow, yet they are sacred to me. My sacredness is real, and so, therefore, is my mourning. I want to teach my children how to love and mourn, because they will need to know how.

According to many a Prius bumper sticker, Chief Seattle (Si'ahl of the Duwamish people) said, "The earth does not belong to us, we belong to the earth." It's a phrase I have heard so many times that I stopped hearing it long ago. As the pandemic unfolded and I watched the cleared patch come up in weeds, the phrase occurred to me in a different light, one without the semi-gloss reflection of my guilt. I no longer saw in it the specter of Admonishment, wagging its personified finger at greed and waste. The phrase itself seemed cleared to the ground and had begun to regrow differently, speaking a far deeper truth, that whatever we do to ourselves and to one another *will* go back into the earth, the soil, that "fund of things." Where else would it all go? That the accumulation of this extraction, pollution, excess, violence, and love *will* become a layer in the layers of the earth. Not because we are terrible beings but *because* we belong to the earth—because we *are* the earth, as a leaf *is* the tree. As the tree *is* the soil and the rain and the sun and, eventually, the soil again. The Anthropocene itself, I realized, may not be the moral judgment I had always read it to be, but a simple and very deep truth, one that calls upon humans to be the best versions of ourselves, but also one that relies on the unshakable stability of a deeper sense of time and place.

Our perception of time may help," said Thich Nhat Hanh in an interview with the *Guardian* at age eighty-six, which he gave two years before suffering a stroke and losing the ability to speak. "For us [death] is very alarming and urgent, but for Mother Earth, if she suffers, she knows she has the power to heal herself even if it takes 100 million years. We think our time on earth is only 100 years, which is why we are impatient." He continues, "Maybe Mother Earth will produce a great being sometime in the next decade . . . we don't know and we cannot predict. Mother Earth is very talented. She has produced Buddhas, bodhisattvas, great beings. We have to accept that the worst can happen; that most of us will die as a species and many other species will die also and Mother Earth will be capable after maybe a few million years to bring us out again and this time wiser."

Solastalgia is what I feel about the wood thrush song, but it is also what I feel when I look at my daughters knowing that the three- and six-year-olds I see and touch will be gone into teenagers, and eventually gone entirely— that the very eyes with which I see them will be gone. When I can release this tension, I can look beyond the anxiety of losing things and can attempt to see my beloveds more clearly. When I am worried about that—if it will happen (it will happen) and when I rail against the fact that it already has happened (those babies, where are they?)—it becomes my anxiety that I see, and not their faces at all. What has happened has happened. What will or won't happen has not yet happened. What can I do now to love them? What can I do now for their world? With acceptance comes resilience and the ability to act. "Come butterfly," Basho sings back, "it's late—we've miles to go together."

Though none of this is mine to keep, what will continue in that fund of soil are my actions; within them my feelings: the anger and gratitude that induce change and also the love, which gives rise and response to grief— which gives form to it. Mourning songs are love songs. I am singing to my children.

The Imprint Theory of Childhood

Jennifer Westerman

A lava flow is a contradiction. A beautiful and destructive unmaking and making of land. It is fire pouring up from within the earth, the red and molten rock puddling and piling, fluid and folding over itself. It is quick popping fountains. Or it is slow movement like a time-lapse of bread dough rising and rolled out, lifting and expanding. Lava flows channel into wide rivers or narrow bands like snakeskins, orange and ashen gray, bright yellow.

In April 2018, the floor of Kīlauea Volcano's Pu'u 'O'o Crater on the Big Island of Hawai'i began to rise and then collapsed. Two days later, the level of the summit lava lake at the Halema'uma'u Crater began to drop. Earthquakes followed, moving along the Eastern Rift Zone. And in early May, fissures opened in Lelani Estates, a residential subdivision in the Puna District. During the first few days, ten fissures opened in backyards and forests, steam rose from road cracks, and noxious sulfur dioxide contaminated the air. Twelve days later, there were twenty fissures, including the impressive Fissure 8. Lava fonts formed and moved southward toward the ocean, rolling over and obliterating homes and habitats, swift with currents and standing waves. By early June, a wide lava delta had formed over Vacationland, another residential neighborhood, and the picturesque Kapoho Tide Pools and parts of Kapoho Bay were submerged beneath new black land. As the lava flow entered the ocean, acrid fumes rose, and fine slivers of volcanic glass fell into the sea.

Nearly five thousand miles away, my husband Jim and I were home in North Carolina obsessively tracking the lava flows. For more than a year, we had been planning to take our family and move for several months to the Big Island. We live on solid granite ground, among old Appalachian Mountains, smothered by shades of green in the summer, painted apple red and burnished orange in the fall, spring an explosion of growth, and winter a long gray sigh. We thought living on an island, even for a short time, would be something akin to the opposite, a horizon defined by water, not rock, by the motion of the sea, not the fixed contours of familiar hills, and by distance, not proximity. We wanted our children to experience new seasons, people, and landscapes, new places, new nature.

For months, Jim had searched for an affordable place to live, and he finally negotiated a discounted long-term stay with the homeowners of a quirky purple bungalow named Hibiscus House. We watched the USGS lava flow maps and the news of residents in the Lower East Rift zone evacuated and then roads cut off. The air became toxic, the water unsafe to drink. And then, the lava flow front hooked northward and then abruptly south and buried Hibiscus House beneath a hot cap of molten rock just a few days before our flight left for the Big Island.

While we watched the devastation of homes and livelihoods unfold, we asked ourselves whether we should still carry out our plans, if we could afford a rental house on the other side of the island, if our presence there would somehow make life more difficult for displaced residents. Would we be irresponsible parents if we chose to take our kids, Iris and Ansel, to the most isolated island chain on earth while a volcano was exploding, earthquakes were occurring daily, and volcanic smog was a gauze across the sky?

Like many parents, we were betting on the imprint theory of childhood. We had added up the years and counted back from eighteen. A work sabbatical for us only came around every six years, and Iris was twelve, Ansel ten. I was already hearing the voices in my head: had I taught them to love the natural world deeply enough? Had we shared enough meaningful experiences, the kind that would someday cause them to become compassionate adults? We still needed to teach them how to iron a shirt. Maybe the lines weren't so direct, but we were betting that the experiences we shared with them as children would leave a planetary engraving on their hearts, a limbic etching extending beyond the earliest stages of life. We were betting that Rachel Carson was right when she wrote in *The Sense of Wonder*, "that for the child, and for the parent seeking to guide him, it is not half so important to *know* as to *feel*." So we pieced together a few rental houses, switched the kids' planned school district, and lowered our expectations for air quality.

Once settled on the island, we listened carefully to the radio, each alert from the reassuring voice of the Hawai'i Civil Defense announcer making us more aware of our surroundings; we watched the color of the afternoon sky to determine if we should stay indoors; and we tested our senses, tasting lychee and lilikoi. Isolation and exposure and low elevation meant something different to us now; we learned how elemental life feels on an island. Trembling earthquakes woke us in the night; torrential rains caused a mudslide, closing the road to school; hot wildfires ran across grasslands like glowing threads in a patchwork garment; and Hurricane Lane tempted the shore, bringing unprecedented rains and flooding to the Big Island. As sea levels rise and surface air temperatures increase, climate models predict extreme weather events will become more common in Hawai'i, rainfall patterns less certain and more severe, perhaps a doubling in frequency of El Niño events, almost certainly diminished trade winds and higher king tides. In the coming years, I know, of course, that Jim and the kids will all be older, and sometimes I forget so will I. The ocean will be warmer then and more acidic as sea surface temperatures rise, the corals we would come to love, imperiled.

I was not young when I became a parent, yet until we lived on the Big Island, I had never witnessed lava flowing, never snorkeled, never been surprised by a dolphin spinning its way toward the surface as I swam nearby, never felt as unmoored. The world below the surface was completely original to me: sunburst yellow tang, black and gold butterfly fish, Picasso triggerfish, a crown-of-thorns sea star. The sea stretched out in all directions was uninterrupted, ongoing in ways I found unsettling and profound. The sky above was darker than a black plum. The stars at night multitudinous. I remember watching my children swimming in the ocean; they were so free, so beautifully alive, Iris's long arms in sweeping arcs, Ansel's lean body in sunlit water. Have you ever felt like crying underwater with a snorkel in your mouth? When they drifted too far away from me, these lifelines, my heart quickened. The ocean was a blue wilderness, enveloping and expansive, and they were there floating, watching, moving through that otherworldly world. They could confidently go on without me, and they did.

Toward the end of our time on the Big Island, my sister came to visit us with her son, Thwaites, who was not quite two years old. I held my nephew on my hip and walked into the ocean. I could feel his legs tighten around my waist. He put his little arm around my neck and pulled himself closer watching the gentle waves with that magic blend of skepticism and curiosity that is the propensity of children. Thwaites held out his hand to touch the water and drew it back, again and again, testing, learning, and he watched my lips intently as I said, "Ocean." He repeated the word to me in a whisper: "Ocean." How I miss those early days. And how I hold out hope that impressions cast in the hearts of children will stir an ecological longing for survival, an ethic of planetary care, an everlasting sense of wonder.

A green sand beach, a cave-like lava tube, the paddling way of sea turtles. Years after our return from the Big Island, Iris and Ansel remember these. They know a lava flow can be generative and ruinous. Ansel remembers canning pickles and making *kaula* cordage from *hau* with his fifth grade class for the crew of the next traditional canoe journey of the Polynesian Voyaging Society. Iris recalls she could hear the ocean from her seventh-grade classroom window. They still remember words to songs sung in Hawai'ian during morning assemblies at their schools, thanking the land for welcoming students to learn *in that place.* They remember sunset hikes with peaceful golden light illuminating the forever expanse of sea, light snow on Mauna Kea, brilliant planets on the black arc of night, and the life (*the life!*) undersea. And when I need to feel a sense of hope in a climate-changed world, I seek what's been pressed upon my memory. I replay the video my sister would later send of my nephew toddling around his Arizona desert home, saying, "Ocean, ocean! Where are you ocean?" I think of verbs synonymous with imprinting—marking, fixing, indelible—and imagine the maps of these children's hearts. They look like lava flows, like blood and veins, life pulsing along toward an infinite blue horizon.

What the Living Do

Erica Cavanagh

The first time my daughter walked toward an ocean, all on her own, not carried in my arms, she was three, in Norfolk, Virginia, tentatively stepping through a tunnel of tall seagrasses until the grasses broke open. Ah! she gasped and bound off laughing, running straight into the water, splashing, and running out as the sea chased her until she turned around and chased the sea back.

I remember this chase from the first time I saw the ocean, too, at three years old, in Pemaquid, Maine. Don't go out of my sight, said Grandma, and I bound off to the tide, amazed at the sea pouring up the shore and pulling back, pouring up and pulling back, ringing around my ankles, and then my stomach as I sat in the rush and retreat of the tide.

I wandered all over that pocket beach, all the way to a seawall of rocks, jutting out into the ocean, and before I climbed, I looked back to see if Grandma could see me. No one else was there, so it was easy to spot her reading the paper, legs crossed at the ankles, and my big brother in red trunks building sandcastles beside her.

I clambered onto the craggy rocks. They were all pocked with puddles, and one puddle that turned out not to be a puddle at all but a deep hollow with barnacles and snails studding the walls and two plum-colored starfish lying on the sandy bottom like sleepy children. I squatted closer. I had never seen starfish before. Something moved in the shadows. I stared at the pool, trying to be still, wondering if I'd seen anything at all, when a crab inched into the light. One step. Two. He seemed to teeter toward a third step, but held still, fixed in a fuzzy sliver of light, the pause pregnant with energy, this way or that way, as if all the stakes in life rested on turning away or venturing forth.

Don't be afraid, I said telepathically. But the crab was wound tight, as guarded as my brother. Slowly, I reached a finger toward the surface to say, See? I'm okay. I won't hurt you. But the crab leapt back into the shadows.

I stared at the pool for a long time, peering into its dark places for a sign of the crab, wanting him to come back, wondering how far the shadows stretched. Maybe there was a tunnel. What if the tunnel stretched all the way to the ocean? I understood the crab had reasons for hiding. To him, I was an invader, and so I lay down, my back against the craggy rocks, imagining secret worlds. A seagull glided in figure eights against the pale sky, and the waves in the rocks echoed through my body. A kind of cathedral calm took over. I was inside the earth's breathing. I was me and more than me. I was small and not small. I had a place in the care of the world, and for a three-year-old girl, that meant *Don't scare the crabs, and if you thought about poking the starfish, don't do that either.*

Grandma got cross when I stayed away too long, so I climbed down and followed the tideline toward the middle of the beach where they sat. I didn't want to leave, and Grandma and Jim didn't appear to be in a hurry, so I stopped along the way, relishing the rush of the waters, waters that held me and let go, held me and let go. I wanted to bring the ocean home and began picking up shells, rinsing each one, and running my finger along the ridges. When an emptied crab shell washed up, face down in the sand, I couldn't quite grasp what it was. Where was the crab? It may have been my first notion of death as meaning *gone,* and I didn't want a single crab, even a dead one, to feel abandoned, so I brought him home.

When Grandma took me into the changing area, helping me out of my wet bathing suit, she scowled. How many times do I have to tell you not to sit in the tide? It's unladylike. She said I got sand in places she wouldn't mention by name. You'll get the car dirty, and your poor grandmother has to clean it up. Once Grandma got going, it was difficult for her to stop. Back in the car she referred to my brother as her prince. He didn't cause her nearly as much trouble, she said. And don't collect crab shells. They stink up the car.

She would really cut into you, my father once said of her.

I grew up at home in nature because whatever nature did, it wasn't personal. Nature was just being itself. Nature did not possess the faculties of reason or prejudice, as humans did, or the ability to reflect on and govern how they treated others. I became a wanderer. Wandering nourished me. Wandering enabled me to cultivate an inner life apart that I carry with me. Almost anywhere, when I am alone and lying still, the ocean rocks me. I am rooted to a place inside me, and that place and I are rooted to Pemaquid and to Grandma, too, as complicated as that may be, and Grandma, or Ruby, as I think of her now, was rooted to Pemaquid, but mostly western Massachusetts, where she lived almost her entire life. Ruby knew the names of all the flowers in Emily Dickinson's garden—lady slippers, foxgloves, zinnias, hollyhocks—and she was proud to live in rural Monson, where Dickinson's mother, Emily Norcross, once lived, and where the Norcross descendants established a wildlife sanctuary, and she, Ruby, established a sanctuary out of the fifteen acres of woods her father bequeathed to her, turning away developers whenever they pressured her to sell the land. She bequeathed these values to her children and grandchildren. Nature tied her to herself. Nature offered her a sense of security that marriage could not, marriage being tied, not to security, but dependence and the degradations of having to ask her husband for money. Nature offered her greater security than being born before women could vote, when a man her young husband admired, a *Mr. Whitney,* she once said bitterly to me, told her husband women couldn't be trusted and to keep her on a short leash. Nature offered her the chance to be unbound, ageless, married to the seasons, making her life larger and more expansive. I carry that too.

In 2003, when I was twenty-nine, I returned to Pemaquid for the first time in two dozen years. I'd lived in many places by then, as far away as Benin as a Peace Corps volunteer. I was having trouble coming back. It was a difficult time to be from here, right after 9/11, when I wished, along with Representative Barbara Lee, "Let us not become the evil we deplore," and instead the U.S. reacted with blind and sweeping vengeance. I wondered if I ever would find a home in this country. Dislocated and heartbroken, I returned to a place I trusted.

At Pemaquid, I couldn't wait to walk out on the rocky outcroppings that bookend the beach only to be surprised to find them covered in massive mops of seaweed. It wasn't like this before, I thought and walked all over the kelp-carpeted rocks, worried I might crush something hiding underneath. There were only a few narrow bald spots where the seaweed parted, but not a single tidepool, only shallow crevices studded with barnacles. I got down and walked along the sides of the rocks, too, looking for starfish and crabs, then crab shells, and found none. It was like arriving at a once-beloved village only to find it abandoned. I returned to the shallow pools with the barnacles and squatted down to look at them. I had never really looked at them before. I'd thought they were inanimate, but they were alive. They moved. The white craters opened and closed like an old man's eyelids, and when they opened, little eyelashes swept out and withdrew, tiny eyelashes, fragile and determined to find food.

We were at the beginning of a massive starfish die-off, mostly on the Pacific coast, but in Rhode Island and Maine, too, from an infectious wasting disease. In the history of the world, disease come and go, but in some areas, this disease hasn't abated for nearly twenty years, killing more stars than previous epidemics. Asked why, scientist Joe Gaydos of University of California, Davis, said, "What we think is that the warm water anomalies made these starfish more susceptible to the disease that was already out there."

In 2020, a *Bangor Daily News* article reported that starfish are making a comeback in Blue Hill, over one hundred miles north of Pemaquid. Scientists wanted citizens' help in counting them. The news should have made me hopeful, but the green crabs and purple starfish that once populated Pemaquid's tidepools remain gone, existing only in my imagination, and as our climate warms, I fear the starfish north of Pemaquid will die again and again only to reappear farther and farther north, gone from the homes that had once been habitable.

I live in Virginia now with my four-year-old daughter. Each summer I take her to Assateague Island off the Eastern Shore. When the waves are long and low, we sit in the tide together, and when we need a break from the sun, we retreat to our beach tent and watch the nickel-sized holes in the sand. Those holes are where ghost crabs have burrowed long, slender tunnels. We watch from off to the side, so we can see how they come out, cautiously, first, as one protruding eye, like an alien periscope, and then two eyes and a few fingerling legs edging out like a child half-hiding behind a door. The crab scuttles back and forth, hide-and-seek style, now you see me, now you don't. My daughter giggles. Why don't the baby crabs come out? she asks. I tell her they're small and we're big. They know they could be trampled or plucked up by a seagull, so they're being careful.

I don't know how she hears the things I say, but I do know, in the words of botanist and writer Robin Wall Kimmerer, that "Being a good mother means teaching your children to care for the world." Observe each life as having a purpose and each life as having something to teach us. My hope is that she'll come to understand that the fate of our mutual lives resides in possessing the humility to measure our scale and possible impact on one another and govern ourselves accordingly.

Back home, after a bath, my daughter plucks her plastic toy crab from the drained tub, puts the crab in a cup, and fills it with water.

"Crabs can't live without water for very long," she tells me.

I smile at my little animist. She's practicing the art of what she could save through care. I wonder a lot about what's salvageable. I wonder if Assateague, a wildlife refuge, will ever be uninhabitable for the creatures who live there now, in its relatively protected terrain, or if its waters will ever be unswimmable, as they were in 2020, our first venture out in the pandemic. I had just stepped from the parking lot onto the beach, pulling my daughter in a thickwheeled wagon, when an old woman turned from her beach chair and said to me, "Don't go out into the water with her. There's sea lice." My grandmother often warned of undertows and child abductors, so I wasn't sure whether to believe her, and what was sea lice anyway? That night, googling at the Airbnb, I learned that sea lice is a common name for jellyfish larvae, and indeed, there was an outbreak of jellyfish larvae close to shore from Maryland down to the Carolinas. Jellyfish are the only sea creatures that thrive in warming waters. All week, I saw beachgoers who presumably did not know, swim out to the shoals, happy, seemingly untouched and basking in the warm August waters, then panicked, rushing back to shore, some of them screaming as they tried to bat the stinging larvae from their bodies.

It is one year later, and I am writing this in the summer when record heat took over the Pacific Northwest. Dead mussels, clams, sea stars, snails, and barnacles blanketed sea rocks from Canada down to Oregon; the mussels split open, their flesh cooked to death. I am writing this the summer when a red tide from fertilizer runoff made the Florida Gulf Coast toxic. Dead fish washed up on shore, an estimated six hundred tons of dead marine life, and a stench that made it difficult for humans and fish alike to breathe. I am writing to you from the summer a friend had to evacuate her kids from camp in Northern California because the Air Quality Index rose over three hundred from a nearby fire. She wrote, "Most of the kids vomited from the smoke." I am writing this from the summer I traveled to Denver to see family. A hazy scrim obscured the Rockies. There were blazes everywhere. The *Denver Post* reported that for the past two years ozone levels have been 48 percent over the federal limit. Dr. James Crooks, a Denver-based climate researcher, said the ozone makes it "relatively dangerous" to go outside from July through October.

On a cool day, when the Colorado fires seemed at bay, my daughter and I walked a wooded trail in the foothills of Conifer with my partner and his family. As we stopped to look at each wildflower, I typed their names in my Notes app: asters, goldenrod, bluebells, yellow snapdragons, yarrow, lupine, buttercups, Indian paintbrush. We used another app to identify the wildflowers we had yet to learn: fireweed, arnica, butter and eggs, nodding onions, wild buckwheat, mariposa lily, wild blanket flower. Grandma Ruby would be right at home in this activity. To document is to cherish. I think of Marie Howe, who, after her brother died, catches a glimpse of her reflection in the window of a store and is "gripped by a cherishing so deep" for her own face. "I am living, I remember you," she says. My cherishing is like that. I record the names to say these flowers were here; we were here—as if that could preserve them—because I know this place could burn.

Choosing a Different Future

Priya Shukla

When I was four years old, my mother enrolled me in Bharatanatyam, an Indian classical dance form. Translated, its name means a "dance that embodies emotions, music, and rhythm." While I was never particularly good (I was slow to learn and never felt motivated to practice), it did teach me the joy of movement. When I opted out of it in adolescence (crushing my mother's dreams in the process), I didn't realize how much of it would stay ingrained in me. I can still do the rapid *dit dit tay* footwork and repeat the mudras (hand gestures) without any prep. But, above all, what has stayed with me is the way we started each session: a short dance to honor the earth we were dancing on, part of which involved gently touching our hands sequentially to the ground, our heads, and our hearts.

Bharatanatyam is India's oldest dance form, dating back to the second century CE. As *devadasis* were performing in royal courts, Jewish people rebelled against the Roman Empire, the Pyramid of the Sun was completed in Teotihuacan, and Hadrian's Wall was constructed in England. Also during this time, lions went extinct in the Balkans, the Lycia earthquake provoked a tsunami that flooded Roman provinces, and the Taupo Volcano eruption in New Zealand turned the sky red across Europe and Asia. Indeed, the stories those dancers told are the same stories I did several centuries later, as walls are erected to separate oppressors from the oppressed, species continue to disappear, and natural disasters have profound impacts that humanity is ill-prepared for.

•

I grew up with my hands in the tide pools of Half Moon Bay (just south of San Francisco), with my father always a step ahead, holding a sea star or some beautiful shell he'd just found. I didn't know the ocean would become my life's work until after he passed away, and I found myself as a student at the University of California, Davis, staring at the bony white skeletons of corals dissolving from ocean acidification. Seeing the effects of increasing ocean acidity from human-emitted greenhouse gases while sitting in a lecture hall with a hundred other students, I still managed to feel alone in this grief. What did it mean to lose a coral reef that neither my father nor I would ever see? Could I help revive the world that my father would never have a chance to explore?

Realizing the direction my career was going, my mother encouraged me to scuba dive. As with Bharatanatyam, I wasn't particularly good, but I rediscovered that sense of movement; the weightlessness of being in the water; that sense of time standing still as you explored the hidden bounty of life beneath the water's surface; the strategic rhythm of breath as you inhale compressed oxygen from your tank and exhale bubbles into the water. Oftentimes, I was anxious as I descended under the water, and I would remind myself to see things through my father's eyes. And so, anxiety, joy, and grief intermingled as I took in every kelp stalk, seashell, and grain of sand I could manage.

I did my last kelp forest dive in 2015 as I was wrapping up a study on how ocean acidification and warming affected the earliest life stages of the charismatic giant kelp that dotted San Diego's coastline. I was used to seeing vibrant, lush, gold-green kelps through which fish would dart. And, where their stalks met the seafloor, you could find highly diverse, thriving communities of invertebrates—from limpet snails to sea cucumbers. But, during this final dive, something felt amiss from the moment I began to submerge. The water was green-gray, obscuring our visibility. As we approached the kelp forest, gelatinous goo seemed to mix with the water. Finally, the kelps themselves came into view, and they were unlike anything I'd seen before, anemic and disintegrating. An unusual Warm Blob of Pacific Ocean water had made it so that we were diving in a kelp graveyard.

Kelps are found in cool, temperate waters where they can reliably acquire sunlight and nutrients. In California, summer is when these two resources are most abundant. However, from 2013 to 2015 the Warm Blob had increased seawater temperatures while driving down the nitrogen and phosphorous kelps require to grow. The unusually warm water circulating through my experiment killed off kelps I was working with in the summer of 2014, though at the time I considered these mistakes borne from my ineptitude as a novice scientist. And at times, even these seemingly devastating concerns evaporated, as the crises under water paled in comparison to those on land: specifically, the killings of Eric Garner and Michael Brown by police during that same summer.

•

Scientists are always told to consider the world objectively. Yet, the fallible, emotional, human aspects of scientists mean our capacity for "objectivity" is limited in scope. After all, it is not objectivity, but structured prejudices that have denied the participation of many marginalized peoples and/or obscured their achievements. Whether it's publishing the double helix's structure without crediting Rosalind Franklin, or building a telescope atop Mauna Kea despite the opposition of Native Hawai'ians to whom that land belongs, or claiming discoveries without crediting the locals who helped explorers safely navigate the terrain and acquire samples. Indeed, some might consider science a sinister endeavor as it often perpetuates sexism, bigotry, racism and colonialism—particularly when applied to humans (e.g., eugenics, phrenology). The brown skin on the back of my hands—which I see every day as I adjust a microscope or count dead oysters—reminds me that the science I do is ensconced in a world designed to work against me and so many others.

Since that dreary kelp forest dive in 2015, I have felt the veil of objectivity continue to dissolve as scientists have been forced to confront their origin stories. Whether they were inspired by the problematic conservationist John Muir or conduct their research in the colonized coral reefs of Guam, carrying these painful truths is critical to studying the planet when it seems we have front-row seats to its demise. It is accepting that the ecological destruction we are both studying and experiencing is couched in greed and violence. And it is acknowledging that as scientists, we have an opportunity to improve our collective future.

•

As my *devadasi* ancestors danced for Indian royalty, they grappled with their own environmental calamities without the means to understand how a far-away volcano could temporarily alter the color of the sky. And, while humans of that era were not responsible for such dramatic environmental change, they were driven by power and ambition; it wouldn't be long before Mughal conquerors razed Indian communities, suppressed their rituals, and enslaved people. In a stark preservation of culture, Bharatanatyam dancers would continue telling those pre-Mughal stories in their artistic way. And today, I find myself tasked with a similar challenge as the world continues to change in extraordinary ways.

Telling our story as we sit on the precipice of climate change is a daunting challenge, but it is also a cathartic one. Instead of choreography, I am using experiments, numbers, graphs, and words. While I've certainly used those tools to track a dying kelp forest, I also use them to document the recovery of a seagrass bed after a storm and the resilience of oysters after a disease outbreak. Unlike the devadasis, I have access to sophisticated instruments and centuries of research to understand how an unprecedented wildfire turned the sky orange across Northern California in the summer of 2020. And, while nothing could have stopped a volcano from doing such a thing, humanity is capable of preventing wildfires from doing so again, at least in the world that will exist beyond me. I take solace in our ability to make choices that benefit us and the people coming after us, while honoring those that came before us.

My father didn't live to see perennial wildfire seasons in California or Hurricane Ida wreak havoc from Mississippi to New York. Nor was he able to see deep-seated nationalism resurge in the developed and developing world alike. While these threats can seem arresting, I remember the joy that nature brought my father, the centuries of turmoil that Bharatanatyam has outlasted, and that, through science and storytelling, I can help us choose a different future. In this decade where we must make significant progress towards managing the effects of climate change, I continue to honor the earth I am working towards preserving by examining it with my bare hands, understanding the consequences of our actions in my head, and feeling propelled to action by my heart. Perhaps future Bharatanatyam dancers will one day tell the story of humanity's superhuman efforts to save the planet and ourselves.

How Do You Feel Today?

Marco Wilkinson

How do you feel today?
I feel the grid of thin plastic threads all welded together to form this bag as
I tear it open to get at the onions inside. I feel the dry skin crack from each
one as I run a knife from stem to root and slip my fingers underneath to
the juicy life within and slide it out of its dead sheath, thinking of my own
skin in middle-age showing signs of wear and dryness encased in clothes
woven of plastic, and I am wondering how to find my way back without
tearing through. I feel powerless to extricate myself from a social fabric that
requires me to artificially wind my life up in oil, even as this container I find
myself in is fraying and tearing everywhere.

How do you feel today?
I feel the silvered bluish-green leaves of the favas growing in my yard and
notice they are finely veined and puckered velvet-soft and rubbery at once
like the soft and tender skin of a scrotum. I feel the pods bulging in ridges
like abs, and there is a subtle shift from one week to the next, from the slight
give of the dewy white foam inside encasing the seeds to the hardness of
maturity and one future butting up tight against the next. I feel turned on
by the ancient accomplishment of agriculture (favas being one of the oldest
of crops) wedded to the pride of knowing my hands laid the seeds into the
ground and watched the first leaves paw out of the earth like green horses'
hooves before galloping to this place of bounty. And I feel ridiculous knowing this minor hero's deed amounts to forty or fifty meals at best. I feel the
grief of original sin when I think of myself as just another seed lined up next

to you in this 10,000-odd-year-old experiment that has been tearing up the ground galloping here to the present and beyond, and that one day when the husk of this fantasy breaks and there is no more municipal water and there is no more neighborliness and there is no more property, no banners of white and black-spotted flowers waving on stalks of silvered blue-green soft and sexy as balls will save me.

How do you feel today?
I feel the wild grapes gleaming hazily black under the thinnest frost of bloom on their skins hanging from vines laced into trees on the side of the trail. I feel spicebush berries shouting in primary red and shining like plastic beads from small understory shrubs whose leaves jab at nostrils with notes of lemon Pledge when crushed. I feel the grainy cranberry-red spheres of Russian olive fruit speckled with silver bursting at every node from these invasive shrubs that are everywhere in these woods. I feel the improbable yellow-pear cherry tomatoes, split after a recent rain, hanging from green limbs entangled into the chain-link fence surrounding the Cargill concrete silos that the trains stop at several times a day. I feel not at all confident that there are enough wild grapes or spicebush berries or even Russian olive fruits for all of us one day when we might need it. I feel unsure about what is in these sidewalk tomatoes but wonder if this is simply karma, that we should ingest what we have sown. I feel the folly of the first cry of "More!" that set you and me on this path (asphalted, shipping-laned, Mars-bound), ravenous and promiscuous like the Russian olives marching across the forests, their arms bursting with children (at least Russian olives fix nitrogen from the air into the ground—what have I ever fixed?). I feel the childishness of playing at foraging the native, the invasive, and the weedy misbegotten climbing out of the ruins, but I hope that this child's play even here in childless middle-age might serve me well when the future demands we all grow up.

How do you feel today?
I feel the keys press down rhythmically under my dancing fingers, digital world indeed where an apple is a computer and a magnifying glass is the universal icon of searching, and after typing in a string of words my index finger slides on the silver rectangle until my digital finger lands on that magnifying glass and my flesh finger taps. I feel the time passing in milliseconds

as the digital magnifying glass focuses beams of electrons through a metal world of wires and an invisible world of waves, neither of which I understand, and I feel the loss of time between now and the last time my flesh fingers, only four years old, gripped a solid magnifying glass and focused beams of sunlight onto a dry leaf in the autumn until it found what it was looking for, that place where the world unknits into flame. I feel pixel fires arrange themselves and knit into a world in front of my eyes and I wonder if this is as close as I can get and I wonder if this will be enough to reweave the fraying edges into a container that might hold me and you. I feel the pity of a thousand ancestors and their guilt at having allowed my fingers to let go of the thread once upon a time as now I watch YouTube videos about weaving hemp ropes in what is currently called Spain and splitting bamboo to weave into baskets in what is currently called China and stripping agave leaves down to their fibers to weave into sandals in Kumeyaay territory in what is currently called Southern California.

How do you feel today?
I feel myself cautiously groping with fingers of light, hoping maybe it's not too late, at a future that I suspect will require a sturdier weave.

One Path to Solastalgia

Paul Bogard

The world, for me, began with water and sky. A lake in northern Minnesota set amid birch and pines, the Milky Way from one horizon to the other. Early, I learned to swim, the water clear and cool, the bottom made of sand. I learned the life that shared that water, the green tiger-stripe perch, the speckled brown ribbons of leech, the legions of minnows flashing silver in the shallows. I was lucky, that's all. My grandfather had grown up on the Iowa prairie, came north once, and never forgot. He and my grandmother began to dream of a cabin near a forest lake. My parents joined that dream, and when I was just able to stand, they built a small house with a screen porch on the second story's southwest corner. I've spent years on that porch watching thunderstorms sweep across the lake, tall pines swirling, lightning revealing a nighttime world—velvet darkness, huge moon, summer's symphony of frog-insect-owl—that imprinted on me. Standing on the dock with my head tilted back was like taking a long, wonderful drink, stars pouring down. What a gift to know that sky as a child, and to carry it through life. Around me were black bear, gray wolf, red fox, moose. Fireflies with their yellow-green lamps, dragonflies with their stained-glass wings, butterflies on wildflower blooms—the world was filled with wild things, and I was one among them.

And the loons. This sleek, red-eyed bird, black and checkered white, sliding from the lake's surface into its depths, racing after its fish. And the call, a long, drawn-out wail that biologists say is a message to its mate asking, "Where are you?" On calm nights that call drifts across the water, echoes in the woods. As a child, I tried to capture those notes on cassette tapes, take them back to the city for winter listening. But the sound out of place was never the same, an early lesson in the difficulty of saving something loved. For a long while—a childhood—all I did was fall in love with this bird, this lake, and the world of which both were part.

I began to see the changes during my teenage years. Driving north I saw the city spread, warehouses and big box stores where open fields of oaks and wildflowers had been. And, at the lake, new house after new house, the starry night fading with ever more lights. By the time I reached college, my knowledge of the world was growing too, of wild places everywhere being paved and cut and burned and plowed. I mourned places I had never visited and now would never know. I mourned as I saw falling population numbers of the storybook animals I'd known as a child—lions and tigers, elephants and bears—their real-world versions disappearing. After college, I chased my rockstar dreams but had inconveniently grown up happy, with a loving family, and now had a stable, longtime girlfriend. I did not have good rock-and-roll material, in other words, so I wrote songs about the animals and birds whose homes were being destroyed. I wished I could make it stop, the insatiable expansion, the constant building, the steady loss of green.

About this time, I found Aldo Leopold's *A Sand County Almanac*, a small book of story and philosophy written by "the father of wildlife ecology" for a lay audience and published in 1949. Seventy-some years ago, Leopold could see the direction we were heading. And while as a scientist and middle-aged man writing in the 1940s he didn't often share his emotions, we know he suffered from a sense of being surrounded by fellow Americans who didn't seem to notice or to care as we humans—we colonizing white humans, especially—wrecked the world that sustains us with food, water, energy, and spirit. "One of the penalties of an ecological education," Leopold wrote, "is that one lives alone in a world of wounds."

I read those words and thought, that's how I feel. I was someone who loved wild places and wild things caught in a society that rewards those who see the planet as theirs to use however they like, an economic system that facilitates the destruction of the natural world, a culture that craves short-term profit over long-term life.

This feeling of being alone has never left me. I know the religious, political, and cultural reasons why people might believe that humans are separate from (and above) the rest of nature, the reasons people seem oblivious as our fellow creatures disappear, the reasons people vote for politicians who in turn vote for ecological ruin. But at some level I just have never understood how people can be this way. Some of me will probably always be the child asking, "Why?"

For Leopold, this feeling of being alone led to a choice. "An ecologist must either harden his shell and make believe that the consequences of science are none of his business," he wrote, "or he must be the doctor who sees the marks of death in a community that believes itself well and does not want to be told otherwise." In other words, we can ignore what scientists are telling us about what we are doing to ourselves, our homes, our children's future, or we can protect, heal, and fight for what we love. Politician, policy maker, parent, poet—if every one of us chose to "be the doctor" in whatever way we know best, what good we could do, what a future we could create.

For me, the choice has always been clear. I can't imagine not trying to "be the doctor" in my own way. And while the feeling of being alone remains, I *know* I'm not alone—the writers in this book are one proof of that. I think now the question isn't how to avoid feeling alone, but rather, how to feel that loneliness while also savoring the joy and wonder still available at every turn.

It's a way of being in the world that I've been learning a lot about lately. Almost four years ago, I became a father. My daughter was born during what sometimes seems like the final years of the world I have known, and the changes predicted for her lifetime are overwhelming. But I knew this when I chose to become a parent. What I didn't know was how being a father would be better than I could imagine, and my love for my daughter greater than any I have felt before.

It's this love that I'm thinking of now, and the epigraph to a favorite book, Jim Harrison's novel *Dalva:* "We loved the earth but could not stay." It works the other way, too: we know we cannot stay, but still, we love the earth. Or, as "solastalgia" would tell us, we cannot stay in the world we love for that world is being radically changed by forces beyond our control . . . and still we love. The question for me—the question solastalgia asks—will be how? What will it mean to love the living world—lake, loons, daughter, and on—when so much of that world is being destroyed?

Of this I am sure: love is the emotion that leads to every other—fear, grief, anger, happiness, joy, hope. It is the emotion to trust and follow as we find our way.

We begin with water and sky, or mountains, or desert, or trees. We begin with animals, or birds, or seasons, or the sea. We stand under stars, absorbing their light. We feel the small hand in our own, the bones like those in a bird's wing fanned, the fragility and the growing strength both. Alive now during this turbulent time, we do what we can and do all we can. We remember what was, imagine what could be, and learn to give thanks again and again.

PART V

Take Action and Take Care

So much depends on what we do now. This includes caring for ourselves.

Step-by-Step Instructions

Janisse Ray

Step 1. Feel.

I lost something precious in a hurricane. Thirty years ago, I put scholarship money down on twelve acres in the Florida Panhandle. I was enrolled at Florida State and had fallen in love with this piece of land, a rare ecosystem called Apalachicola steephead. It was remnant Appalachia, way down in North Florida, growing extant rhododendron, trout lily, and trillium.

Paying off Sycamore, as the place was called, took years. Then there were property taxes, every year. I kept paying, because my dad had drilled into me that having a home was a person's best security and because I wanted the old-growth beech and magnolia to keep masting and sheltering, breathing in carbon dioxide and breathing out oxygen. I couldn't save the world, but I could save one leafy bluesy greensy breezy place.

In October 2018, as Hurricane Michael cannonballed Mexico Beach, Florida, I worried about Sycamore, two hours north. I waited two weeks to go check on it.

I've seen the aftermath of many hurricanes. When I saw Mexico Beach, however, I knew that Michael was different. The word that comes to me is "displacement." Dunes were in the ocean. The ocean was in the houses. A bathhouse was sideways in the dunes. Sand buried the boat ramp. Trees crushed houses they shaded. One house had come to rest on a tree. Boats were stranded on high ground, one at the grocery as if parked there. A ballcap hung from the broken limb of a tree. A pelican's wing dangled useless.

The broken road was a tunnel passing through mountains of detritus—ruined appliances and furniture, soggy mattresses and carpets, sections of dock and boardwalk, tree trunks and limbs.

Michael was a compact storm. A tight knot at its center had wreaked Godzilla damage, a new Category-5 kind of malice. But the fireball of Michael's eye had not cooled once it devoured the coast. It punched north up the Panhandle at Category 3, a bowling ball, an axe.

In Sycamore twisters had spawned on the forested slopes. Ninety percent of mature trees were down. Loblolly, beech, and hickory, some with trunks three feet wide, crisscrossed in tangles. Michael had done something I would never do. It laid Sycamore to the ground. The blood in my veins reversed course and knocked me down.

Accept the problem in its severity, Good Grief Network says. *Sit with uncertainty. Feel your feelings. Grieve for a future that will be more parched, more wet, more crowded, more dangerous, more austere.*

Step 2. Quit.

The person hardest hit will not be me or you, people with privilege—it will be a mother living in poverty in a shack in a country outside the U.S. There are times when feeling, especially grieving, prevents us from being part of the solution. Some years ago, an EMT from my community responded to multiple tornadoes that killed many people in Alabama. When she returned, she reported people sitting in the crisis shelters "rocking themselves back and forth," a shock response that is understandable, sometimes unavoidable, but also potentially treacherous, in that it disables a victim from addressing a current moment's needs. We can train ourselves to lessen the chance of going into shock.

Step 3. Shift.

A moment came in my life when grief dropped its intolerable weight on me. I had been a divorced and single mom for a decade. The decisions I'd made, many of them poor ones, weighed heavily on me. When my son went to live with his father, I was thrown deep into grief. "You cry if a leaf falls," someone said to me.

I made an appointment with a therapist I could call the world's best without hyperbole, the late Charlie Kreiner, whose work I knew from co-counseling, a movement whose core mission was world change through personal change. The session began and so did the tears. If Charlie said, "You were born," I wept. Charlie said it was old stuff, restimulation. He said I had so much available grief that I could get seduced by it. The goal of therapy is not to cry, he said. It's to change your life. "This is about being creatively empowered to take on the work of history," were his exact words.

He advised me to assess my life, look at life-goals, and get very clear about what I wanted. "Lay a foundation for what you need to know is true in order to live the life of your dreams."

"To survive rising temperatures," Jonathan Franzen wrote in *What If We Stopped Pretending?* "every system, whether of the natural world or of the human world, will need to be as strong and healthy as we can make it." Bill McKibben, the great climate activist, said, "The best antidote to feeling powerless is activism. It doesn't make you less sad, but adds hope, solidarity and love."

Shift from feeling to action.

Set yourself up in a life as sustainable as possible. Build a belief in your own resilience. Boost your preparedness. Prepare to do without. Prepare to travel less. Sell your car. Prepare that big ag is not going to feed you. Start growing food. Learn to cook. Go as long as you can without shopping. Build to withstand extremes. Don't build a new house. Restore an old property. Install unit-based solar with no grid hookup. Dig a well. Decarbonize your economy. Use recycled wood. Learn to carve. Recycle paper. Actively create a support network. Have people over. Cook for them. Go on a walk with them. Host a tree walk. Go plant trees. Celebrate a birth or a birthday with a new tree. Give a tree as a wedding gift. For Christmas, not only buy trees for friends and family but plant them. Stop mowing so much. Cancel a flight. Stay home. Connect to your place. Lobby for federal logging restrictions. Fundraise to buy a vacant lot for an orchard. Buy a clearcut outside town and replant it. Buy a forest and save it. Protest a tree being cut. Put up a tree swing. Share the stories.

Step 4. Realize.

During the pandemic I signed up for an online summit with Thomas Hubl, self-described mystic and healer who studies how societies heal from collective tragedies like the Holocaust. I wanted to think about this, since we find ourselves in multiple collective tragedies—the pandemic and the climate emergency to name two. During a free-write Hubl asked participants to answer the question, "Who am I in relation to the world and the changing climate?"

Who am I? I am the dark void of disbelief. I am shreds and tatters. I am the one who desires to add no harm, not even a kilowatt of energy. I am the desire to plant trees.

Collective grief seems to be the compilation of vast personal griefs. But collective grief is not the sum of individual griefs. A third entity, a miasma larger than all of us, is created.

Step 5. Work.

Collective grief, as with personal grief, is seductive, especially in a culture that sets so much store by personal identity, personal threat, and personal affront and that too often substitutes rhetorical change for real change. We are in charge of our individual healing, but collective healing takes leadership.

Part of our collective grief has been years of dishonesty on the part of our leaders, the ways they have lied to us reinforcing our lies to ourselves:

—by not digging into the data
—by implying uncertainty in the data
—by being mistrustful of science
—by unlinking humans from causation
—by being too eager to rest in "optimism bias"
—by hesitating to explore the bad news
—by, on the other hand, allowing themselves to become pessimistic
—by implying that we have plenty of time
—by forgiving self-destructive behaviors

Good leadership means telling the truth. Good leadership requires open, fair communication. Good leadership needs input, involving women and people of color and the poor and the rich and men. Good leadership rewards innovation, vision, heroism, and other good leaders. Good leadership provides manageable, effective acts most of us can manage—the victory garden, the shoebox project, the hybrid car. Good leadership apologizes. Good leadership empathizes. Good leadership is tender-hearted. Good leadership insists on wisdom, even when the media, the bots, and the influencers bully wisdom, elders, and wise elders.

Collective healing requires justice. The justice can be symbolic. In fact, collective healing requires symbols and monuments, places we can take our grief and rage and feel that we are being heard.

Step 6. Heal.

If personal grief is healed through personal action, collective grief must be healed through collective action. This is one reason policy change is so important. First, it is substantive change. It solves problems faster: a person choosing to ride a bicycle makes a small difference; lowering vehicle emission standards makes a big difference. And actions that affect the multitudes facilitate collective healing.

Heal collective grief through collective action.

Set impossible annual caps on carbon, methane, and other greenhouse gas emissions. Tax emissions. Ration carbon. Set tough standards for efficiency on refurbishments, new-home construction, appliances, lighting, air cooling and heating, and any item that uses electricity or fossil fuels. Bring manufacturing back to the United States. Ban wasteful technologies like patio heaters and garden floodlights. Outlaw new roadbuilding and road-widening. Freeze airport construction. Ban mountaintop removal. Stop the construction of new power plants. Teach conservation standards in school. Build a community resilience project. Make yours a Transition Town. Upgrade the US rail system. Illegalize any logging happening on roadsides. Severely limit or ban corporate industrial logging. Immediately employ massive tree-planting programs. Plant a trillion trees.

Step 7. Feel.

How to Love a Burning World

Jennifer Atkinson

When you live in Seattle, a city known for its rain and gloom, summer is the season of redemption—the big payoff after endless winter gray. Or at least it used to be. In recent years our anticipation of blue skies and clear mountain views has been overtaken by dread of wildfire season, when smoke drives us inside and brown skies block out the sun. As one long-time resident here remarked, "I used to wait for summer to cure my seasonal affective disorder, but now I have it in July and August too."

Even smaller aggravations—the ubiquitous smell of smoke, itchy throats, and red eyes—have become unbearable in light of the knowledge that one is breathing the scorched remains of forests and animals, lost homes and human lives, and toxic particles from a thousand untraceable sources: cars and sofas and laptops and buildings.

And then there's the heat. A week before I wrote these words, the Pacific Northwest experienced the highest temperatures ever recorded in Seattle, Portland, and parts of western Canada, which soared to 121 degrees Fahrenheit. Scientists said it was a one-in-a-thousand-year event. Roads became so hot they literally buckled. And hundreds died in a region where most of us do not have air conditioning. To put this all into perspective: the average June high in these parts is 69 degrees.

And yet the misery of this heat intensifies another feeling that doesn't subside when the temperatures do: a deep, existential dread of all the summers ahead. As Charlie Warzel wrote in an op-ed following this June from hell: "there's a distinct psychological pain that accompanies the thought that the unbearable present is only a preview of the extreme climate to come."

This sensation stretches far beyond our region, of course. Eco-anxiety, climate grief, solastalgia—call it what you will, the American Psychological Association defines the general phenomenon as a "chronic fear of environmental doom." In a recent survey of people ages eight to sixteen, nearly three-quarters reported being deeply worried about the state of the planet—and such numbers are rising across every age group. My own students at the University of Washington tell me they have nightmares about the future or don't want to have kids because they believe the world is hurtling toward apocalypse. As they've watched snow disappear from our mountains and salmon decline in our rivers, their distress has grown so intense that I launched a seminar to help students cope with climate despair.

So is this rise in anxiety good or bad for the planet?

It depends. On the one hand, climate despair can depoliticize our environmental crisis. When we pathologize eco-anxiety as if it were some kind of mental health disorder, we locate the problem with the individual rather than the larger political structure. And that directs our focus toward soothing people's feelings instead of taking collective action to overhaul the systems turning Earth into an ashtray. I often see this among students who enroll in my climate grief seminar hoping the program will "fix" them so they can go back to feeling happy. It's understandable to want relief from this pain: but in doing so, are we seeking solutions to the wrong problem?

Moreover, while climate anxiety may be an effective "wakeup call" for people initially learning about climate injustice, staying in a space of alarm, panic, and dysregulation can be counterproductive in the long term. This is especially true among climate activists and those already deeply concerned. At best, constant fear and stress lead to burnout. At worst, they drain our courage and immobilize us from acting in the first place. Mental health professionals also point out that such emotions trigger the fight-flight-or-freeze response, overriding the kinds of creative and critical thinking we need to work through this crisis. And in the face of an existential threat like climate breakdown, personal anxiety can quickly spiral into helplessness, nihilism, and despair—all of which fuel a too-common belief that we're too insignificant to impact the situation. It also doesn't help that people who feel depressed and isolated are more likely to withdraw than to seek out others—the very thing needed in this critical moment for building coalitions and taking collective action.

Yet on the other hand, we mustn't dismiss the truth of our pain, which arises from a profound love for all that's being destroyed. Grief is a sign of compassion and connection with the living world. What would it mean *not* to mourn all this lost beauty, the humans and wild creatures that won't survive the upheavals to come, and the suffering that didn't have to happen?

When we suppress our grief for the world, we're also suppressing our compassion for it.

This recognition—that love is actually the source of our pain—may be the key insight needed to navigate the contradictions of climate despair. As Malkia Devich-Cyril has written, "Joy is not the opposite of grief. Grief is the opposite of indifference." Having lost my father to cancer the same year I began teaching seminars on climate grief, I learned how these links can offer a pathway through personal bereavement and the loss of nature alike. With both, we discover that grief is not here to take us hostage; grief is a guide, showing us the root of what it is we love and deepening our resolve to protect it. In the face of accelerating climate upheaval, this insight has served to remind me that I'm not a hand-wringing alarmist but a human being with a working emotional compass that points my attention to what matters most.

Honoring this link between love and eco-grief can have political benefits as well. We'll never address our climate crisis without a critical mass engaging the political process, and that requires us to transcend self-focus, seek out others who feel urgency and concern as we do, and then work in concert toward a common goal. Love is essential to that process because love directs our attention outward. At its core, love is an affirmation of something beyond the self—a desire to act on behalf of another being. Even a planet.

None of this means we'll feel cheerful across the years ahead. On the contrary. Our love for the world is the very thing that brings pain as we witness so much life and beauty destroyed.

But that grief is never the whole story, and looking only at our losses perpetuates a self-defeating myth that nothing of use has ever been achieved and that all the work lies ahead. And so we must also tell the story of what remains and how that came to be. The trees on our streets that were not cut down because someone a generation ago fought to protect them. The pockets of wildlife starting to recover because past activists changed the laws.

The air and water that is cleaner than it would be, the species that have not been driven to extinction, because people last century passed legislation to protect them. All that still thrives, all that was not destroyed, because someone once loved it.

Harnessing both love and grief, it's our turn to be those people to future generations.

This Will Be

Elena Passarello

One morning last September, my smoke alarm sounded at 4 a.m. It turned out the sound wasn't an alarm, but rather the robo-cricket chirp of the device nearing its end. And when I rose to silence it, I saw the smoke alarm hadn't made the noise at all: it was the other plastic square plugged into the wall—the one that monitors carbon dioxide.

Still, when I recount that morning, I always say "my smoke alarm died" because it happened during the time that my house was surrounded by both alarms and smoke. In the eight summers I'd spent in my little Oregon community, I'd learned the side effects that fires from the Cascades can bring—hazy days, red sunsets, even flakes of ash in the air. But those summers were nothing like what happened in 2020, when anomalous winds blew in from the east, knocking down power lines and spreading several fires that burned unprecedentedly close to my home. Thanks to reduced snowmelt, the Oregon ground was exceptionally dry that year, though perhaps "exception" is not the truest word for this anymore.

These fires had names people spoke with quick familiarity, reminding me of the hurricane-prone months of my childhood in coastal South Carolina: another region beset with late-summer worry. In September 1985, a Category-3 storm with my first name forced our kindergarten class into lockdown; we ducked and covered in the hallway and a girl hissed at me, *"This is all your fault!"* I remember the strobing emergency lights and my teacher's face, unable to mask its concern.

By Labor Day 2020, fires surrounded my town on three sides, the closest one about thirty miles Northeast. The radio knew what was coming and sounded its own alarm, as did my cellular provider and cable company. Tuesday evening, my neighbors sat at the top of our street and watched the sky turn orange—the last sunset we saw for nearly two weeks. The birds stopped singing, and the air hazard level shot past any extant metric. No air on the planet was more dangerous to breathe, the radio said. Our outdoor plants were flecked with ash, which also covered cars, porches, windowsills. A haze seeped into my house and floated like chemtrails near the ceiling. But we knew we had it so much easier than people in nearby communities who were evacuated to my town's camping areas and motels, all stuck here until it was safe to return to what remained of their homes. It struck me more than once that the ash and smoke surrounding my house *was* their homes, so who the hell was I to complain.

I kept the cats inside, sealed the windows, and spent the first days glued to my phone, scouring local listservs for calls to help. I Venmoed restaurants so they could open their kitchens and feed evacuees and hauled water and linens to church drives. But more than anything, the emergency taught me how useless I was—how totally unprepared. I was the kid in the hallway, covering her neck with her feeble hands again. At one desperate point, while I stared out the window at the hazy outlines of deer in my gray front yard and wondering if they were thirsty, I filled two overturned frisbees with hose water and put them on the driveway, where they just gathered ash for days until I sheepishly retrieved them.

The radio taught me the state alarm system's three levels of warning: Ready (prep to evacuate), Set (stay crouched to leave at a moment's notice), and Go (run the fuck out the door). I stuffed a bag with cat food, chargers, and fiber bars and placed it in the foyer, where my husband tripped over it constantly. The Internet, which taught me how to pack that bag, called it varied monikers of alarm: the survival pack, the bug-out bag, the trauma kit.

All of us were woozy from the air in our house. We spent our time drinking bourbon (humans) and dozing (felines). I soothed myself with Elvis movies because none of their plots involve wildfire, though "Hunka Hunka Burning Love" somehow bored itself into my head and lingered. This is how it goes inside my brain. The anxiety of the days, coupled with inactivity, stoked so much maudlin thinking, which I suppressed by mainlining pop culture because it pulls my attention like a magnet.

Most pop songs, no matter their subjects, are designed to exist in the everyday. Pop radio might shift between songs of heartbreak or elation or vengeance, but these topics are sung at a low-grade intensity appropriate for your dentist's office. This ubiquity can turn spooky when pop songs underscore moments of crisis. Martin Scorsese figured this out early in his film career, and I felt it about halfway through the weeks of smoke and ash, when I couldn't postpone a supermarket trip any longer. Walking through the glass doors, I heard the in-store radio system blaring REM's "It's the End of the World as We Know It." When I texted about it to my friend in Atlanta, who had been checking in since my town made national news, she quipped back, "at least it wasn't 'We Didn't Start the Fire.'"

A few mornings later, my smoke alarm—which was really the carbon dioxide alarm—went off. I'd say it sounded before dawn, but there was no real dawn that day. A chirp and then a long pause, long enough to make me distrust my hearing, before another chirp. I woke my husband and brought the unplugged detector into our bed for him to inspect. The back of the plastic device clearly described the chirping as its deactivation cry. Not a scream of poison in the air, but the swan song of planned obsolescence. "See?" he said.

The many alarms of the past weeks left me unconvinced. I lay back down and spent an hour trying to snuff racing thoughts about the house, the vulnerable creatures inside it, all the harms I hadn't the skills to detect or repair. My phone said Home Depot opened in a half-hour; here was something I could do. "It can wait!" my husband groaned, but I found shorts and flip flops, put a jacket over my nightshirt, and grabbed the car keys.

All the other vehicles in the lot at six a.m. were work trucks—pros, I assumed, getting a jump start on their days. Even in the middle of a disaster, pipes still burst; toilets still exploded. The detectors sat on an outfacing shelf near the flooring center, and I stared at them for twenty-five minutes. I couldn't judge the differences between the fifteen-dollar detector and the model three times as expensive. Their boxes shouted urgent phrases at me: "WORRY FREE!" "LONG LIFE!" "SMART HOME!" I returned to the car, hustling through the queasy air with an armful of options.

A week into the fire emergency I banned the car radio as an act of self-preservation, switching to Spotify. A wonderful writer who is also deeply wed to pop music had been making epic, five-hour playlists during the pandemic—each one covered a year in music from the late sixties to the early aughts. I had worked through them up to his 1975 mix, a year whose summer also burned with disaster. Bushfires destroyed 450,000 square miles across Australia, killing tens of thousands of animals (six of them human) and burning 15 percent of the continent. Hurricane Eloise flooded the Gulf Coast and made landfall with 115 mph winds. Among the notable songs from that year: "Makin' the Best of a Bad Situation," "Someone Saved My Life Tonight," and "Emotional Weather."

As I drove through the smoke with my brand-new alarms, the 1975 mix played Fela Kuti. Olivia Newton-John sang "all I need is the air that I breathe" at a stoplight while I watched a masked attendant blast the 7-Eleven's sidewalks with a leaf blower. Dionne Warwick crooned about burning bridges when my car rolled past the fairgrounds, which were filled with the tents and RVs of the displaced. And as I crested the hill into my neighborhood—usually a summer scene of variegated greens, blackberries, and Smurf-blue sky—the playlist began Natalie Cole's "This Will Be."

Hearing this song in grocery stores never made me bat an eye. Light and adaptable, I knew it in myriad pop contexts, from Christian dating service ads to the Lindsay Lohan *Parent Trap* reboot. I recognized this song right away, at its pickup measure: three sixteenth notes on a loosely tuned church piano, backed by four clapping hands. Then the organ, strings, and Cole's bright voice seep into the rhythm, and the melody rises like alpenglow.

"This Will Be" is a pop song about how it feels to be loved. Or maybe, rather, it voices the very moment a person realizes that love has found her, that love is packed into the very air she inhales to sing each lyric. The song takes the discovery and runs with it—spreading, expanding, eating all the oxygen it finds. Verses jump over measures like each was a highway, absolutely refusing containment. I once watched a contestant in a televised drag queen competition offer a high-voltage lip sync of the song. She saved herself from elimination by kicking and dipping and shaking her pageboy wig at every beat, every blare of the horns. That morning in my car, the song conjured her: the astonishing scene of her body becoming sound and story all at once. A body that knows just what to do in order to stay vital: it must become that joyful noise.

The final third of "This Will Be" is a series of giddy repetitions. Cole's lead vocal and the backup vox shout together in blaring fifths, refusing perfect intonation as the song dances offstage in a run of echoed phrases. "You're so deserving!" is sung three times, then "yeah!" four times, and the lyric "from now on!" ten times, plus once more for good measure. But the most repeated word of the outro is "love." A monosyllable the same size as "fire," with the same typed vowels as "smoke," that carries an altogether different profile when in its sonic form.

Cole's repeated singing of "love" just sent me on that horrible brown morning. Who would ever think to put such power in a kiddie movie or a produce aisle? Her voice made love a counter to the smoke and the dread and the darkness. Love, her voice announced, could be its own kind of alarm, when it's belted into the rotten air with the trumpeting insistence of a dawn chorus. Again and again and again—eighteen damn times in a row—it sounded: "LOVE! LOVE! LOVE! LOVE! LOVE! LOVE! LOVE! LOVE! LOVE! LOVE! LOVE! LOVE! LOVE! LOVE! LOVE! LOVE! LOVE! LOVE!"

I pulled my car over to the bike lane and sobbed.

On Time

TAYLOR BRORBY

1

I was born to a world in need of more time. When I was butter bean new-born in western North Dakota, barely seven months old, the *New York Times* reported that James Hansen told a Congressional committee that NASA was "99 percent certain that the warming trend was not a natural variation but was caused by a buildup of carbon dioxide and other artificial gases in the atmosphere."

Seven years later, while watching *Rocko's Modern Life*, my favorite cartoon about a wallaby, the residents of Rocko's fictional O-town learned about fluorocarbons in the atmosphere. Captain Compost Heap, a pile of muck oozing around O-town, educated residents that because of the pollution from Conglom-O, the local factory, the ozone was being eaten away by the fluorocarbons.

I stared out my own living room window and saw smoke puffing from the stack of the coal-fired power plant where my mother worked.

When I left for college at eighteen, hydraulic fracking ripped across western North Dakota, plunging the prairie with pipe to tap the previously difficult-to-reach reservoirs of oil in the Bakken shale play.

During my first semester in graduate school in Iowa, when I was twenty-seven, the *Des Moines Register* announced that one of the world's largest pipelines would carry twenty-four million gallons of oil from western North Dakota, through Story County, where I was living at the time, to Patoka,

Illinois, every day. From there, it would shoot the oil south to the Gulf, where it would then be refined and sold on the world market.

Now, at thirty-three, my eyes are again focused on my home power plant in western North Dakota to see if Project Tundra will signal to the world that carbon capture and storage—the pumping of liquified coal and ethanol emissions over a mile underground, where it will supposedly stay forever—is a *go*.

There is no end to capitalism's appetite for destruction.

2

For most of my writing life, well-intentioned friends advise me to *slow down*, to *take my time*. But when you grow up in a world without time, and when your childhood was paid for by coal, there's not only an impending sense of not having time, but also of responsibility. For years I wrote op-eds about the oil boom ravaging my home in western North Dakota, the least-visited state in the country. I wrote literary pieces for journals. I traveled to colleges and universities to speak about what I had seen when I lived in the oil boom. I coedited an anthology of creative writers to speak against fracking across the country. I wrote and wrote and wrote.

And, finally, while in graduate school in Iowa. I blocked construction equipment for the Dakota Access Pipeline and was arrested in August 2021.

What else should I have done?

We live in a world where the ocean is on fire, where Mount Shasta is without snow.

We live in a world where my fragile prairie is torn apart.

3

As a child, whenever I was caught with a book, my parents would tell me to *go and do something*. Though I wanted to stay lost in the pages with *The Boxcar Children*, or to tremble through the *Goosebumps* books, what my parents gifted me was a relationship with the wide world western North Dakota—how iridescent clam shells shimmered in the shallow Square Butte Creek, how my eye was trained to trace the trail of muskrat through water, to notice the difference between a pheasant and grouse cry. Or—to run like hell if a badger barreled at me.

4

To notice is demanding work. To stand one's ground is demanding too. But work is all I know; it seems to be all I can do in the face of everything I understand about the mess we're in—and the one we're moving deeper into. I am not focused on stopping "climate change," whatever that nondescript, umbrella term is—"climate change" has not moved me to act. But the destruction of my prairie has—the ripping apart of switchgrass, little bluestem, and bunchgrass roots—the ruin of Native American sacred sites, the pollution of the Missouri River. My responsibility as a beneficiary of the coal industry who grew up in a trailer house in a county without a stoplight, as I see it, is to write like hell, because the body of the earth—and my own body, ravaged from diabetes—is under immense duress. It is a pleasure I'm not afforded—*to slow down, take my time.* The future, in the context of my life, is not bright, but that does not mean I don't think I can put up a damn good fight in the meantime.

5

The other month I was interviewed about the Dakota Access Pipeline Wars by an undergraduate student in Illinois. She asked me what the basic thing people needed to understand about what moved me to act against the Dakota Access Pipeline. I took a moment before speaking. And then I said this: The Dakota Access Pipeline is a simple, one-dimensional, violent story: it is a story of destruction. My story against the Dakota Access Pipeline is not only *mine* but also a tapestry of stories threaded together—of coalitions from North Dakota and Iowa joining together, of farmers standing their ground, getting arrested to protect their precious topsoil. Native Americans blasted with watercannons in frigid North Dakota. Grandmas raising hell in Iowa. It was that my individual story was not a solitary story: it was a story in community.

6

In a time of such immense grief and catastrophe, one of the few things that helps me get out of bed, put on my socks, and get to it is the sheer fact that that's what I have to do—get to it. It's not to believe that only recycling, or becoming vegan, or driving less is actually going to do much in the grand scheme of things (other than maybe make me feel smug). It's rolling up my sleeves, hitching my work to others, and letting it rip to try to transform the shoddy systems we've been handed—and that looks like a lot more community work than just little old me sitting by myself, only putting pen to paper. For me, it's showing up to townhall meetings, getting comfortable with being uncomfortable and, at the end of the day, asking one simple question: How can I help?

Why Turn Inward Just as the Planet Needs Us Most?

SARAH JAQUETTE RAY

There's a lot of talk these days about the urgency of our moment, about acting like our "house is on fire," and how the moment is so pressing that there's no time for anything other than action. Even in the flurry of discourse around climate emotions, all the rage is to talk about how emotions are pathways to action, how action alleviates anxiety, and so on. The fetishization of action, the appeal to the risk-perceiving limbic system, and the call to make bigger impacts, faster, are backed by science. The latest IPCC report, not to mention the fact that more and more of us are experiencing climate change in our daily lives, has brought climate change to the forefront of our worries. We've gone from mass denial to mass dread and trauma. Systems-level change, and in a hurry, certainly seems to be the correct response to what we are experiencing.

Yet, I want to propose the perhaps counterintuitive idea that the wisest response may actually be to slow down and go small. I propose that the trope of urgency and the related imperative to go big can undermine our best intentions and burn us out. I would even say that these pressures are part of the root cause of our climate problems in the first place.

Paradoxically, in this moment of urgency and crisis, what we need most is the ability to slow down and resist the myriad ways that the productivist imaginary of capitalism shows up in our daily practices. Every single moment of our attention is precious, every single way we spend our time matters, and every habit we start adds up over time to the response-ability that these unfolding, layered crises will require of us.

I'm not suggesting that we escape the pain of the external world by devoting our energy to only comforting ourselves. Much like swiping, doomscrolling, or seeking some other form of numbing for our pain, one can just dive into a navel-gazing approach to self-care that harms others even more. When we numb ourselves to our interior lives, we make it hard to feel any emotions deeply, seeking the dopamine hits of distraction to keep trying to feel alive. Ironically, the more we do this, the less connected to each other and the world we become, and the more harm we do to other life on the planet. Instead, pain can be an invitation to cherish the world and to experience the satisfaction available to us in understanding suffering as tenderness toward that which we love.

Our current model of capitalism, which doesn't take into account the environmental and human costs of growth, conspires with our negativity bias to put us on the back foot, constantly *reacting* to immediate stimuli, rather than building life-enhancing structures in the first place. It has us scrambling to put out fires as they come rather than address the causes of the fires—literal and figurative—in the first place. Likewise, we have come to rely on those in power to save us rather than build resilient communities.

Urgency is a recipe for burnout and for doing more harm out of reactivity, while the expectation of large-scale impact is a recipe for feeling powerlessness and despair. We can limit capitalism's power to work through us, in small and slow ways that reduce harm—*right now*. By slowing down, by focusing on the small, I'm not suggesting that large-scale actions aren't required, or that we aren't living in an urgent moment. I'm asking us to embrace the paradox that the only way we will survive this together is to recover our amygdalas, cultivate practices that pause between stimulus and reaction so we can act more wisely, and to find pleasure in our capacities to make a difference in the scale that we live in every day—the human scale. Faster, quicker, and bigger are capitalist values that got us into these problems in the first place and would have us exhausted by chasing one crisis to the next. The planet needs us to pay attention to our interconnectedness to the material world and each other, and act wisely in service of protecting that relationship. Turning inward doesn't mean turning away.

One way we can act wisely is to act from a place of abundance, rather than scarcity and fear. When we show up to the work that is needed from a place of abundance, we have more energy and time to give, and are wiser about the places and people we give to. We simply cannot do everything that is needed, and so we have to make choices about where to dedicate our limited energy and attention. But when we doomscroll or go down other rabbit holes in our social media, we allow much of that energy and attention to be hijacked in service of the very source of harm we worry about.

Why do we bypass inner work in times of crisis? In times of crisis, many of us may be tempted to think, "There is no time for self-care; the work is urgent." But in times of crisis, there is no cushion for making mistakes. We do more damage when we impulsively respond to each other and to threats based on whatever our nervous system tells us to do. Fight, flight, and freeze are often unwise reactions, and they can do as much harm as good. Inaction is not wasteful, and it's not even inaction. Pausing helps us to proactively anticipate the least harmful actions and to proceed responseably. This is why Bayo Akomolafe writes, "Oh, the times are urgent. Let us slow down."

We must be intimate with our interior lives because we want to have our own thoughts and act in alignment with them. We don't want capitalism thinking (and subsequently acting) through us. Capitalism limits our vision for what's possible. It makes us think we're powerless to do anything, framing our challenges as predetermined and unavoidable, or too big for us to make any difference. It likes us to think that our agency is constrained to that unit capitalism likes the most: the consumer. And our sense of our worthiness is attached to the thing that capitalism rewards most: our role in the treadmill of production—our careers or incomes. Capitalism makes us feel urgent and busy, too busy to take care of relationships, the land, and ourselves. And like capitalism, we then externalize the costs of this busyness elsewhere—the planet, our loved ones, and our livers, our immune systems, and other organs, to say nothing of the more-than-human world and all the species with which we share it.

Finally, in slowing down, we can own up to the ways we do harm in the world, disrupt the habits of distraction and denial that extend these harms, and feel the grief that is appropriate to the losses we are witnessing and undergoing. We must dispense with our fetishes of size and scale—the myth that we are worthless if we don't make big impacts and fast.

If, in fighting against the forces that are killing us, we ourselves diminish life, we have done their work for them. We can't wait until the revolution is over to live the life we are fighting to save; living it *now* is an act of resistance itself.

I sympathize with my students, who are so impatient about changing the world that they can hardly sit in their seats long enough to finish a discussion about an article, much less work on projects or, sin of all sins, sit and do nothing. Action is cathartic for them. And I am the first to measure my own worth by my sense of being busy. My default is to assume that if I'm not exhausted, then I'm not working hard enough to be a good ancestor to future generations.

Since the pandemic, I have taken a closer look at how my relationship with time is connected to my relationship with the more-than-human world, and with other people around me. In the name of career success, I have avoided response-ability in my daily life, seeking convenience over interbeing, large over small, "impact" over reverence, and outrage and burnout over equanimity. The painful irony is that I have wasted so much time, missed so much beauty, and done so much harm in the pursuit of "saving the world."

But action without wisdom perpetuates the problem. In June 2020, I dusted off my meditation and mindfulness practices out of sheer necessity. I was beside myself with grief, despair, exhaustion, and anxiety. In the intervening months, I have come to realize that the best I can do in my brief time on this earth is to do as little harm as possible, starting with what is right in front of me. There is no other way to figure out how to do this besides sitting still and doing nothing.

Smoke, Cracked Corn, and a Helicopter Rescue

ALISON HAWTHORNE DEMING

Excessive heat warning, a high pressure kettled over the Southwest. It has been a summer of record high temperatures. Heading to 113 degrees in Tucson as I write this. Death Valley climbing to 130 degrees, the hottest temperature on Earth. California farmers are quitting, selling water rather than crops. Cherries are shriveling on the branch in the Pacific Northwest. Young salmon in the Sacramento River dying off in the heat. Cold-water-loving trout dying in Montana streams. The Southwest megadrought may be the worst in 1200 years. Lake Mead and Lake Powell, reservoirs "that made the Southwest plausible" as Joan Didion wrote, have the lowest water level in their history. And when the rains come, they are so extreme the ground can't absorb the deluge. Fire ravaged land erodes, slips, and slides. Brooks and streams and washes roil into torrents. Entire villages in Germany swept away. Subway tunnels in China and New York City inundated. Sea water seeping into the foundations of Florida homes and condo complexes. Rebar and concrete corroding. The entire game of cards crumbling. The search for survivors called off as attention turns to an approaching hurricane. Meanwhile, pandemic rages, sparking in hot spots all over the world. Science tries its best to get the facts into people's minds. Distrust runs so deep that even a simple answer to a complex problem fails to be taken seriously. Meanwhile, democracy is being dismantled, state by state, as new laws are put in place to deprive the majority their right to vote, a despicable power play fueled with lies.

So I walk the dog early, mountains hovered with smoke from the Telegraph fire that burns near Globe one-hundred miles north of Tucson or the

Woodward fire that burns in the Huachucas sixty miles south of Tucson. We name the wildfires as if they were our children. My nose and throat rasp from the smoke. Eyes water. The body knows where we are at. The dog is filled with joy on her slow sniffing walk, taking in the scent of the night's visitors: javelina, bobcat, packrat, king snake. She gobbles up mesquite pods and nuzzles into a scattering of jojoba beans that have fallen to the gravel. Her head jolts up at the call of a crow. She feigns a lunge toward a foraging finch, surprised as always when it takes flight. After rain, the ocotillos sprout sleeves of fancy green. The dog tucks her nose into a claret cup cactus blossom. She seems to find every flower delicious. When the sniffing is done, she cleaves to my side as companion in the feast of all that is. Amidst this evidence of life's determination to thrive, it is impossible not to feel joy. This is the paradox of all life: peril and joy walk hand in hand.

Last year at this time the Bighorn fire came within a mile of my house in the Catalina foothills. It burned for forty-eight days, raving through 120,000 acres of forest and scrub (small in comparison to fires raging this summer in Oregon and beyond). The blaze drove wildlife down from their mountain refuge. I caught the image of a huge six-point buck on the wildlife camera I had attached to a patio chair in my backyard. I was trying to figure out who was stealing my lettuce and swiss chard. The mule deer had to cross a four-lane city street, meander through a close-knit suburban neighborhood, and leap a four-foot brick wall to land beside my little cement birdbath. After a few slurps, he turned to nibble on a Texas Ranger shrub, then spotted the salad bar. Imagine his joy to find that tender forage after a season of bristle and spine in the Sonoran Desert. He gorged and left nothing but nubbins. I was pissed and yet . . . how could I begrudge such wiles, such animal joy?

Fire crews worked night and day to tame the beast that flamed from west to east. At night I'd go outside to watch how the orange seam traced the fire's rampage along the ridgeline, moving on after consuming the available fuel. The fire crews spoke of it as if it were alive. "We turned it . . ." "We're prepared to engage if it begins to move down from the ridgeline . . ." "We've created a defensible perimeter . . ." It was eerie. It was sublime, that spectacle of natural force. The mountain range that looked so impassive most days revealed itself to be an organism capable of feeling. It seemed to suffer, as we saw it, though forest scientists say the fires cleanse the land, open new browse for the animals, crack wide seeds that had waited years for this cataclysm to trigger germination. It was terrible and beautiful. Neighbors met at night on the streets, eyes lifted, go-bags packed, nervous conversation stitching us together.

So what am I feeling? I suppose I feel that constellation of feelings which does not have a name: vulnerable, scared, sad, pissed off. Climate dismay. Climate anxiety. Alienated from myself as member of a species so adept at self-justification that it does not have the will to stop what U.S. Climate Envoy John Kerry has called "the world's mutual suicide pact." The fact that we are all complicit is one of many conversation stoppers. What can we do? Stop driving? Not have kids? Is there any ground for hope? Friends ask these questions with a resigned shrug. It's as if any action would by its nature cause harm. The darkest alley this thinking can take us down was exemplified for me recently by a man who insisted, "The best thing I can do for the earth is to kill myself." Suicide pact indeed. But I find hope in the fact that after saying this the man rose from the table on his deck and walked to the edge of the woods to scatter cracked corn for the Chihuahuan ravens that had drawn near his house. Every good deed is a pact with life.

Solastalgia is too pretty a word for this monkey fist of emotion. It means homesickness for a sense of place that is lost. A sense of belonging. A sense of a plausible future. In the music of the word I hear solace in the first two syllables drowning out pain in the last three. Or maybe the pain is reflexive, wiping out the solace that preceded it. It's a beautiful and complicated word that insists upon a both/and relationship between pain and solace rather than an either/or. In a both/and world, borders are zones of exchange not of exclusion. In a both/and world, the fact that we are all complicit in planetary destruction obligates us all to work on repair. Complicit in destruction, complicit in repair. Each within our capacity and field of influence.

If you make policy, make it just and sustainable. If you make bread, make an extra loaf for someone in need. If you make a garden, don't lace it with poison that kills the pollinators your garden requires. If you fear for the future, tell someone you love about your fear and let them share the burden, then together make one choice that contributes to repair. If you are in a book club, forget that new romance and instead read *Fifty Simple Things You Can Do to Save the Earth* or, for the more ambitious, *Drawdown: The Most Comprehensive Plan Ever Proposed to Reverse Global Warming*. Then do one thing the book urges you toward. It's not too late to prevent the worst possible outcomes. Yes, the changes are coming harder and faster than predicted. Almost but not quite too late.

I don't know what to say to those among us who cling to denial, rather than taking up the challenge of repair, who argue about the Big Lie and Mr. Potato Head while shopping for more guns, who think liberty means I can kill you if I don't like what you say. Is all of this mendacity and denial and cruelty a deflection of the fear and vulnerability that climate change inflicts? Get over the outrage, folks, and plant some trees. Pick up a shovel and build a check dam to keep the flood waters at bay. Pick up some solar panels. This is real. This is now. Speak out for the lions, for the bees, for the butterflies, for the elephants who have gone on walkabout in their own solastalgia for a disappearing world. Speak out for the dispossessed of all species including our own. Speak out for the human soul, which is growing wizened and mean when we need it most to be magnanimous and in love with the miracle of our existence, to be protective of the conditions on Earth that made us and all the more-than-human world possible. This is our work, the Great Work, in Thomas Berry's immortal words.

I was coming home from the hardware store one day at the end of the wettest July ever in Tucson—over eight inches in one month. Annual rainfall here is estimated at around 10 inches per year—but we haven't come close to that for the past two years. Climate weirdness. This July extreme rains dumped over seventeen inches of rain in the higher regions on the Santa Catalinas and the water had nowhere to go but downhill. I stopped to take a look at the Rillito, the river that runs through our city, though it is almost always dry. It's thrilling when the river rolls. People line up on its banks as if the flow were an athletic event. So I wasn't surprised to find the parking lot and the railing on the river walk lined with gawkers. I was surprised to see two EMTs loaded with emergency kits climb out of a fire truck and head for the crowd.

The river was a racing tumult of muddy water, swirls and eddies and backsplash, indeed a spectacle for desert dwellers. Two guys had been inspired by the river's exuberance to toss their kayaks in and paddle their way to mastery over nature. Nature had another idea. And if the guys had scouted just a hundred yards downstream, they would have seen that idea take form in the monstrous hydraulic that would suck them under where water cascaded over a low dam. The EMTs had an easy time pulling the first guy and his boat out. I saw him standing under his upright kayak as if it was some sort of rustic shelter. He was soaked and bore a sheepish countenance as the EMT questioned him. Who knew where his partner-in-folly was? A heavy-built middle-aged guy told me he'd seen him go under in the churn. He must have been under for at least fifteen seconds. When he came up he was limp, floating downstream as if he had no arms. He said he'd run a mile along the river walk to keep the capsized guy in his sights. He'd been the one to call 911, and I could see that he was hyped with the hope of a rescue.

The spectators were rivetted, all lined up at the rail and exchanging snippets of story as they'd come to understand it. No one said, "What a fucking idiot to go into the flood waters," though most of us must have thought it. All of us said, "I hope he's alive." We saw the crew head for a weedy island in the midst of the flood, but there was no way to reach the stranded kayaker. By now there were emergency crews on both sides of the river. A fierce ethic of care rippled through the crowd of spectators. The sheriff's helicopter arrived, circled, hovered, and lowered a man from the craft bearing a rescue ring. Then the cable was pulled back into the chopper, the two men held in an airborne embrace, the kayaker hanging like a wounded bird, lofted to safety.

I'd like to think of this story as a parable. When an emergency is clear, people join together in an ethic of care. All they want is for the vulnerable one to live. Just for a moment, they do not judge or argue or allow themselves to be distracted from the reality before their eyes. Not everyone wades out into the floodwaters to make the rescue. But the attention paid is a kind of communion of souls we rarely see in our divisive time. I'd like to think of this story as springboard for a thought experiment. Would we do a better job at taking on the climate emergency if we told ourselves that everything we love is in dire jeopardy unless we pay attention, call in the emergency crew, show each other that we care more about the vulnerable than we care about our differences? I'd like to pretend that it is so and that in pretending we practice the act of radical imagination the crisis demands.

Fireflies

SCOTT RUSSELL SANDERS

During the 1950s, in the rural pocket of Ohio where I grew up, kids would often gather on summer evenings in a hayfield or scruffy yard to make a lightning bug lantern. When it was my turn to host, I supplied a mason jar with holes punched in the lid, and a net cobbled together from cheesecloth, a loop of fence wire, and a stick. On instructions from my mother, who didn't want us killing fireflies, we stuffed a few fresh leaves and a damp wash cloth in the jar. Then we waited, twitchy from anticipation.

As dark came on, one or two tiny lights began flashing among the tall grasses, and soon there were dozens, then hundreds, and on the grandest nights maybe thousands—as many fireflies, it seemed, as stars in the sky. One kid held the mason jar, ready to lift the lid and then set it quickly back in place. Another kid swept the net through the swirl of fireflies, catching several with each stroke, and then gently shook them into the jar. Once we had a jarful, we circled around to stare into the blinking galaxy.

On those nights when the gathering took place behind my house, I got to keep the lantern, which gave off enough light for me to read by in bed. I sat propped up on pillows, glancing back and forth between the page and the glittering jar. When I grew too sleepy for reading, I went outside to release the fireflies among the grasses where we had caught them, so they could go about their lives. I didn't want our game to cause a single one to die.

Today, you can still find hayfields and scruffy yards in the northeastern corner of Ohio, and also in southern Indiana where I have spent my adult life, but on summer nights you will see precious few fireflies. Where there used to be hundreds or thousands of flashing lights, now there may be a handful or none at all. Evenings in June and July seem emptier without them. My children and grandchildren can peer into the glowing screens of cellphones, laptops, and sundry other devices, but they have never made a lightning bug lantern.

This might not strike you as much of a loss, in an age well supplied with entertainments. We have plenty of electric lights to break up the darkness, indoors and out. But consider that these mere bugs—which are in fact beetles, belonging to the largest order of insects—evolved a means of signaling to partners and predators by generating photons, like miniature suns, and they do so without producing any waste heat, without burning fossil fuel, without drawing electricity from wall sockets, batteries, solar panels, or nuclear reactors. Wonder at this achievement should be reason enough to lament the vanishing of fireflies. Add to wonder the fact that the light-emitting compound they created, called luciferin, is now being used in medical research, gene sequencing, drug development, brain imaging, and in the search for signs of life on the moon and Mars. Shouldn't simple prudence, as well as gratitude, prompt us to feel alarmed by the disappearance of such a useful creature?

Year by year these tiny suns are winking out, and not only here in the Midwest. There are more than 150 species of fireflies in North America, more than 2,000 worldwide, all diverging from a common ancestor roughly 100 million years ago, and everywhere on Earth their numbers are diminishing. The reasons for this decline are not entirely known, but the factors we do know about—pollution, habitat loss, and global heating—are also causing declines among all classes of insects, animals, and plants. For instance, wildlife surveys reveal that populations of fish, birds, mammals, and other vertebrates have been reduced, on average, more than 50 percent over the past half century.

The prime factor driving the collapse of so many of our fellow species is rapid growth in our own. In 1951, when I first chased fireflies with a homemade net, the human population numbered just under 2.6 billion; in 2021, as I write these lines, the total has surpassed 7.9 billion, a threefold increase within a single lifetime. As our population swells, the habitat available for other species shrinks. Our towns and cities sprawl. We carve up the countryside with roads. We dam rivers. To grow more food, we fell forests, plow grasslands, drain wetlands, and empty aquifers; we scour the seas to catch more fish. As marine stocks plummet, we build gigantic trawlers that scrape the ocean floor bare; as we erode topsoil, we dump ever-increasing amounts of fertilizer made from natural gas, using up fossil fuel and adding to greenhouse emissions; as monocrops attract pests and diseases, we spray more poisons, which seep into streams and reservoirs, and eventually into our bodies. And still, despite all this damage, nearly a billion humans go hungry, and millions more lack a place to sleep in safety.

In addition to suffering from pesticides, loss of habitat, and climate upheaval, firefly populations are dwindling worldwide due to light pollution, which drowns out their flashes and disrupts their mating. Imagine how many human romances would fail if phone service broke down. The same electric glare that bewilders fireflies also dims our view of the stars, enclosing us more tightly in the bubble we have manufactured to shield ourselves from the rest of nature. Lately, the bubble has been cracking, letting in floods and droughts, wildfires and hurricanes, drug-resistant microbes and epidemic diseases. On every continent, human refugees are on the move, more of them each year, fleeing environmental disasters and the wars fomented by those disasters.

In our efforts to enslave the whole of Earth to serve humans, we have made it less hospitable not only for ourselves but also for millions of other species. The crash of firefly populations is just one illustration of this debacle. A similar story could be told about drastic declines or extinctions among frogs, migratory songbirds, salmon, butterflies, bumble bees, cheetahs, chimpanzees, sedges, redwoods, longleaf pines, tortoises, sea turtles, orcas, sage grouse, and any number of other creatures.

For over three billion years, evolution has been weaving the web of life on Earth, linking all creatures, from bacteria to humpback whales, into vital relationships—pollinators to plants, plants to grazing animals, grazers to predators, predators to scavengers, scavengers to microbes, and so on through every level of complexity. We humans, latecomers to this pageant, are tearing the web to shreds. For the most part, we are not doing so maliciously, but carelessly, ignorantly, selfishly. Like other animals, we are following instinct and appetite. But unlike other animals, we have developed the technological means to multiply our population and amplify our actions beyond all biological constraints. Now that spree is ending, as we outstrip Earth's supply of crucial resources, such as fresh water and forests, and we exceed Earth's capacity for absorbing our wastes, such as greenhouse gases in the atmosphere, plastics in the oceans, and toxins in the soil.

In cultures shaped by otherworldly religions and equipped with powerful tools, we may be lulled into thinking that humans are separate from the
rest of nature, that our fate is not bound up with that of fireflies, warblers,
and wolves. But this is an illusion, as long-lasting Indigenous cultures have
always known. We do not dwell outside of nature. We are woven into the
web of life, and as it frays, our lives, our cities, our societies also begin to
unravel. Knowing this, knowing how much of Earth's abundance we have
squandered, we are bound to feel dismay and grief. But we must not sink
beyond grief to despair, for if we dismiss all efforts to undo the damage as
futile, we will betray our children and future generations, along with our
fellow species.

As an antidote to despair, consider once again the creativity of nature
manifested in fireflies. Luciferin, their light-emitting compound, is made
from atoms of carbon, nitrogen, sulfur, oxygen, and hydrogen; except for
hydrogen, every one of those elements was forged in the interior of stars that
burned out or exploded billions of years ago. So those miniature suns that
captivate children on summer evenings are fashioned from the remnants
of actual suns. If nature can create such beauty from cosmic debris, what
might we, as channelers of that creativity, be able to accomplish? We can
replant forests, clean up rivers, restore prairies and wetlands, draw energy
from wind and sun, grow food without poisons, and coax endangered species back from the edge of extinction. This work is already underway, in
communities and watersheds around the world, carried on by people com-
mitted to preserving and mending Earth's living web. Whatever our age or
circumstances, wherever we live, however much or little time and effort we
can devote, this is the work we are called to do.

CONTRIBUTORS

GLENN ALBRECHT is an honorary associate in the School of Geo-Sciences, the University of Sydney, New South Wales, Australia. He retired as professor of sustainability, Murdoch University, in mid-2014. He continues to work as an environmental philosopher and published his book *Earth Emotions* in 2019. He currently lives at Wallaby Farm on Wonnarua land in New South Wales. His most recent work develops the meme of the "Symbiocene," a future state where humans reintegrate with the rest of nature.

LAUREN K. ALLEYNE is the author of two poetry collections, *Difficult Fruit* and *Honeyfish*, as well as coeditor of *Furious Flower: Seeding the Future of African American Poetry*. Her work has appeared in the *New York Times*, the *Atlantic*, and many other publications. Born and raised in Trinidad and Tobago, Alleyne resides in Harrisonburg, Virginia, where she is a professor of English at James Madison University, and the executive director of the Furious Flower Poetry Center.

JENNIFER ATKINSON is an associate professor of environmental humanities at the University of Washington, Bothell, and creator of *"Facing It,"* a podcast exploring climate grief. Jennifer leads seminars on climate and mental health across North America in partnership with activists, artists, psychologists, and climate scientists.

CYNTHIA BELMONT is professor of English and gender and women's studies at Northland College in Ashland, Wisconsin, where she teaches creative writing, literature, and intersections in gender studies and environmentalism. Her essays have appeared in *River Teeth, Harpur Palate, Hawaii Pacific Review*, and other journals.

PAUL BOGARD is the author of *The End of Night* and *The Ground Beneath Us,* both from Little, Brown, and *To Know a Starry Night* from the University of

Nevada Press. He teaches writing, literature, and environmental studies at Hamline University in Saint Paul, Minnesota.

TAYLOR BRORBY is the author of *Boys and Oil, Crude,* and *Coming Alive: Action and Civil Disobedience.* He is a contributing editor at *North American Review* and serves on the editorial boards of terrain.org and Hub City Press.

NICKOLE BROWN is the author of several books including *Sister, Fanny Says, To Those Who Were Our First Gods,* and *The Donkey Elegies.* Spruce Books of Penguin Random House recently published *Write It! 100 Poetry Prompts to Inspire,* a book she coauthored with her wife, Jessica Jacobs, and they regularly teach writing workshops as part of their SunJune Literary Collaborative. She lives in Asheville, North Carolina, where she volunteers at several animal sanctuaries.

ERICA CAVANAGH grew up in Rochester, New York, and served in the Peace Corps in Benin. Her writing has appeared in the *Missouri Review, North American Review, Bellevue Literary Review, Off Assignment,* the *Journal,* and elsewhere. She teaches at James Madison University.

SUSAN CLAYTON is a professor of psychology and environmental studies at the College of Wooster. She studies people's relationships with the natural world and how they are socially constructed. Most recently she has looked at climate anxiety and other psychological impacts of climate change. Her edited books include *Identity and the Natural Environment* and *Psychology and Climate Change.*

ALISON HAWTHORNE DEMING'S most recent nonfiction book is *A Woven World: On Fashion, Fishermen, and the Sardine Dress.* Author of five nonfiction books and five poetry collections, including *Zoologies: On Animals and the Human Spirit* and *Stairway to Heaven,* she is regents professor emerita at the University of Arizona. She lives in Tucson and on Grand Manan Island, New Brunswick, Canada.

LAURA ERIN ENGLAND is an ecologist and environmental communicator who teaches in the Department of Sustainable Development at Appalachian State University. She pours her climate concern into leadership of cross-campus climate literacy efforts such as the Climate Stories Collaborative and the Climate Responses and Response-Ability initiative.

BEN GOLDFARB is the author of *Eager: The Surprising, Secret Life of Beavers and Why They Matter,* winner of the PEN/E.O. Wilson Literary Science Writing Award. His work has appeared in the *Atlantic, National Geographic, Orion Magazine, Smithsonian, Mother Jones,* and many other publications. His next book, on the developing science of road ecology, will be published by W. W. Norton & Company.

LEAH NAOMI GREEN is the author of *The More Extravagant Feast,* winner of the Walt Whitman Award of the Academy of American Poets. Her work, which has appeared in the *Paris Review, Orion,* and elsewhere, has received a Lucille Clifton Legacy Award and an AAP Treehouse Climate Action Poetry Prize. Green teaches at Washington and Lee University and lives in Rockbridge County, Virginia, where she and her family homestead and grow or find much of their food for the year.

GENEVIEVE GUENTHER is affiliate faculty at The New School and the founder and director of End Climate Silence. Her next book, *The Language of Climate Politics,* is forthcoming with Oxford University Press.

KEN HADA, a poet and literary ecologist, is a professor at East Central University in Ada, Oklahoma. His two recent books are *Contour Feathers* and *Sunlight & Cedar.* Information about his work can be found at kenhada.org

HOLLY HAWORTH's work appears in *Orion,* the *New York Times Magazine, Oxford American,* and elsewhere. Her essays have been listed as notable in *The Best American Travel Writing* and included in *The Best American Science and Nature Writing.* She currently lives in the Georgia Piedmont.

DOUGLAS HAYNES is the author of *Every Day We Live Is the Future: Surviving in a City of Disasters* and *Last Word,* a chapbook of poetry. He teaches writing and environmental humanities at the University of Wisconsin, Oshkosh. He lives in Madison, Wisconsin, with his wife and two daughters.

SEAN HILL is the author of the poetry collections *Dangerous Goods* and *Blood Ties & Brown Liquor.* His numerous awards include fellowships from the Cave Canem Foundation, Stanford University, and the National Endowment for the Arts, and his poems and essays have appeared in numerous journals and anthologies. Hill is an assistant professor in the creative writing program at the University of Montana and lives in southwestern Montana with his family.

JOAN NAVIYUK KANE's most recent book is *Dark Traffic.* She has received a Guggenheim Fellowship, a Whiting Writer's Award, an American Book Award, the United States Artists Creative Vision Award, and the Donald Hall Prize. A lecturer in the department of Race, Colonialism and Diaspora at Tufts, she also teaches creative writing at Harvard, Tufts, and the Institute of American Indian Arts.

J. DREW LANHAM is a distinguished alumni professor of cultural ornithology at Clemson University and poet laureate of Edgefield, South Carolina. He is intensely rural, progressively southern, and tending feral. Drew is the author of the award-winning autobiography *The Home Place: Memoirs of a Colored Man's*

Love Affair with Nature and *Sparrow Envy: Field Guide to Birds and Lesser Beasts*. He resides in the Upstate portion of South Carolina formerly known as "The Dark Corner" in the shadow of the Blue Wall.

KATHRYN MILES is the author of five books including *Trailed: One Woman's Quest to Solve the Shenandoah Murders*. Her work has appeared in *Audubon*, *Best American Essays*, the *New York Times*, *Politico*, and *Time*.

KATHLEEN DEAN MOORE is a philosopher, environmental activist, and award-winning nature writer. Among her many books are *Riverwalking, Pine Island Paradox, Great Tide Rising*, and now *Bearing Witness: The Human Rights Case against Fracking and Climate Change*. She writes from Corvallis, Oregon, and from a cabin where two creeks and a bear trail meet a tidal cove in Southeast Alaska.

KATHRYN NUERNBERGER's latest book is *The Witch of Eye*, which is about witches and witch trials. She is also the author of the poetry collections, *RUE, The End of Pink*, and *Rag & Bone*, as well as a collection of lyric essays, *Brief Interviews with the Romantic Past*. She teaches poetry and nonfiction for the MFA program at the University of Minnesota.

ELENA PASSARELLO is the author of two collections: *Let Me Clear My Throat* and *Animals Strike Curious Poses*. Her recent essays have appeared in *Audubon, National Geographic, Mcsweeney's*, and *Paris Review*. She teaches in the MFA programs at Vermont College of Fine Arts and Oregon State University and appears weekly on the nationally syndicated radio program Live Wire!

ANGELA PELSTER's first essay collection *Limber* won the Great Lakes Colleges Association award for best new book in nonfiction and was a finalist for the PEN award for the Art of the Essay. Her new book, *The Entanglements*, is forthcoming with Mad Creek Books. She lives and teaches in St. Paul, Minnesota.

ROOPALI PHADKE is professor and chair of environmental studies at Macalester College, where she has taught since 2005. Her teaching and research focus on energy and climate policy, citizen science, and community-based research. She lives in St. Paul, Minnesota, with her husband and three children.

JANISSE RAY is an American writer whose work often inhabits the borderland of nature and culture. She has published a dozen books, including *Ecology of a Cracker Childhood*, a *New York Times* Notable, and *Wild Spectacle: Seeking Wonders in a World beyond Humans*. She has won an American Book Award, Pushcart Prize, Southern Bookseller Awards, Southern Environmental Law Center Writing Awards, and Eisenberg Award, among others, and has been inducted into the Georgia Writers Hall of Fame. Ray lives and works near Savannah, Georgia.

SARAH JACQUETTE RAY is chair and professor of environmental studies at Humboldt State University in Wiyot territory, also known as Arcata, California. In addition to coediting three volumes on the intersection of the environmental humanities and social justice, Ray is the author of *A Field Guide to Climate Anxiety: How to Keep Your Cool on a Warming Planet.*

SUZANNE ROBERTS's books include *Animal Bodies: On Death, Desire, and Other Difficulties, Bad Tourist: Misadventures in Love and Travel, Almost Somewhere: Twenty-Eight Days on the John Muir Trail,* and four collections of poetry. She lives in South Lake Tahoe, California.

SCOTT RUSSELL SANDERS is the author of more than twenty books of fiction and nonfiction, including *Hunting for Hope* and *A Conservationist Manifesto.* His latest book, *The Way of Imagination,* was published recently by Counterpoint Press. An emeritus professor of English at Indiana University, he lives in the hardwood hill country of the Ohio Valley.

PRIYA SHUKLA is an ocean and climate scientist currently pursuing a PhD at the University of California, Davis. She also a contributor for *Forbes* and the Currently weather service. Follow her on social media @priyology.

MEERA SUBRAMANIAN is an award-winning independent journalist, author of *A River Runs Again: India's Natural World in Crisis* and a contributing editor of *Orion* magazine. Based on a glacial moraine on the edge of the Atlantic, she's a perpetual wanderer who can't stop planting perennials. You can find her at www.meerasub.org.

JENNIFER WESTERMAN is associate professor and chair in the Sustainable Development Department at Appalachian State University. She is coeditor of the journal *ISLE: Interdisciplinary Studies in Literature and Environment.* She is currently at work on a book of essays, *The Limits of Hope,* about parenting and climate change in Southern Appalachia.

MARCO WILKINSON has been a horticulturist, farmer, and editor, in addition to being a professor of creative writing and sustainable agriculture. He is an assistant professor of literary arts and cultural studies in the literature department at UC San Diego, focusing on creative nonfiction and eco-writing. He is the author of *Madder: A Memoir in Weeds.*

PRISCILLA SOLIS YBARRA is a writer and associate professor in the Department of English at the University of North Texas. Her publications include *Writing the Goodlife: Mexican American Literature and the Environment* and *Latinx Environmentalisms: Place, Justice, and the Decolonial.* She is currently Clements senior fellow for the study of southwestern America at Southern Methodist University.